**Fiberglass Boat
Survey Manual**

Fiberglass Boat
Survey Manual

Arthur Edmunds

John de Graff, Inc.
1979

John de Graff, Inc.
Clinton Corners, N.Y. 12514

Printed in the United States of America.

Contents

List of Photographs

List of Figures

CHAPTER 1

The Boat Owner and the Surveyor

Everyone needs to have confidence in his boat and its equipment. Unless all systems are in good working order, you certainly don't want to take your family offshore, where a failure of the hull or fittings could be disastrous. Even if you only go for short outings in protected waters, you want to be sure your boat is in good condition for the safety of everyone aboard.

Hiring the services of a marine surveyor when you purchase a boat and periodically thereafter can help you maintain confidence in its seaworthiness. On the basis of his inspection, the surveyor will report any deficiencies, providing information that is invaluable to you as boat owner and that is usually required by your insurance company as well. Even if you are very experienced and like to inspect your boat thoroughly from time to time, it is always good to have a reassuring second opinion, as all of us can miss a detail now and then.

This book is designed to give both the professional surveyor and the boat owner an increased measure of confidence in their abilities to inspect a boat and determine what needs immediate repair. The emphasis is on fiberglass, as the vast majority of modern hulls are built of this material, primarily because the molding techniques lend themselves to relatively low costs in large-volume manufacturing.

Briefly, the glass material will be described and the design criteria outlined, but without detailed discussion of design and construction factors that are required only by the naval architect. It should be emphasized that the responsibilities of the designer and the surveyor are quite separate and distinct; the function of the surveyor is to

9

inspect the condition of the boat and not necessarily to evaluate its design or the construction techniques that have been employed in its manufacture. In fact, it may be well to define a survey as an inspection of a boat and a statement of its condition at the time the inspection was made.

The surveyor applies specialized knowledge and a practiced technique to each marine inspection. Two observers may look at the same section of hull or at identical sections of piping and comment on different details, or neither may notice anything worth mentioning. The surveyor, however, knows where to look, what to look for, and the implications of what he finds. When he inspects an area of fiberglass hull, wood joinerwork, or a piping system, for example, he asks himself whether the material has been selected properly and whether the part in question has been fabricated correctly as an integral part of the boat.

In short, the surveyor depends on his experience with many boats and his knowledge of recommended boatbuilding practices in order to examine a boat thoroughly and determine the state of repair, or lack of it. Of course, no book can substitute for experience with many different boats, but this one points the owner in the right direction and shows him where to look for problems.

Perhaps the most difficult task for a surveyor is attempting to know all the strengths and weaknesses of particular pieces of equipment that have been added to the basic boat. It is difficult if not impossible to describe the hundreds of varieties of marine equipment in a survey manual, and only the basic systems will be discussed here. In the case of such equipment as radios, navigational gear, electronic indicators, heating and air conditioning, windlasses, and autopilots, both the owner and the surveyor would do well to rely on the specialized advice of an experienced repairman if the survey shows that such gear is not functioning.

Choosing a Surveyor

The boat owner naturally wants to hire the best possible surveyor, one who is experienced and who will aggressively search the boat down to the smallest detail. There are many ways of locating a good surveyor, but the inexperienced and/or prospective boat owner will usually do best by following the recommendation of his insurance agent. After all, the insurance underwriter has to make good on any losses and he, too, needs the advice of a good surveyor to determine the potential risk the boat may present. Usually you can also expect the yacht broker, boatyard, or marina to have a list of surveyors they have called on in the past and found to be reliable.

However you select a potential surveyor for your boat, it is best to have a frank discussion with him right away. Tell him about any problems or questions that have arisen, and make sure he is prepared to investigate them. For example, a particular surveyor may not be familiar with aluminum or ferrocement construction, or he may survey only powerboats, or if he does look at sailboats he may not go up the mast in a bosun's chair to inspect the spreaders and masthead fittings. Be sure you hire a surveyor who can examine *your* boat properly. In any case, a detailed list of questions at the start will prevent a great deal of misunderstanding later on.

It is important for everyone concerned to recognize that a surveyor is only human—that he may fail to uncover a leaking pipe fitting or a frayed electrical wire during the course of the inspection. Most complaints against surveyors come from boat owners who find a frozen seacock or an electrical short just a few months after receiving a survey report that did not list it as a problem. True, the surveyor may have missed the deficiency, but it is also very possible that the problem did not exist at the time of the survey. Further, a problem may be hidden behind a permanent installation so that a surveyor could not have detected it. In short, the surveyor can inspect only those areas of the boat that he can see, and his job is to report the condition of the boat at the time he sees it.

The cost of a survey is usually a very small portion of your investment in a boat. The price is certainly reasonable when weighed against the safety risks presented by a boat in poor repair—to say nothing of the financial risk of purchasing an unfit craft that may generate unanticipated yard bills. In fact, the surveyor's fee may very well be less than the boatyard charges for hauling and launch-

11

ing, and no survey can be complete unless the boat is out of the water. Some surveyors charge four or five dollars per foot of boat length for a normal survey, but be prepared for additional fees if you require sea trials, an engine mechanic, or special attention to a particular piece of equipment. Other surveyors charge a flat fee of $200 per day, or they charge hourly on the basis of travel time, waiting for the boat to be hauled out of the water, and fulfilling the extra requirements of the owner. Whatever the surveyor charges, good advice is worth every penny of the fee.

The owner should watch the survey and talk to the surveyor when he is finished to gain as much information as possible about his boat or the boat he intends to buy. A personal conversation with the surveyor, often during a quick lunch, will go a long way to increase the flow of necessary information. The owner, or prospective buyer, should make every effort to be present when the survey is undertaken. Although the surveyor will do a professional job in any case, he will naturally give less personalized attention to an owner who doesn't even bother to visit the boatyard. Of course, it doesn't improve relations to look at every detail over the surveyor's shoulder either, but he does appreciate the owner's concern about specific problems, and he will supply answers to a prepared list of questions concerning areas of suspected trouble or equipment that is known to be faulty. If a prospective owner is unsure about certain areas of the hull, he should definitely question the surveyor in order to get a professional opinion, unbiased by a desire to sell the boat or related marine equipment.

The surveyor has an important part in the selection of a new boat in addition to his role in determining the state of repair of an older one. Usually only the surveyor or another boat owner will give a direct, honest opinion of the qualities of a new production boat, although a friendly boat broker will have vast experience with used boats and can tell you whether a certain model has withstood the test of time.

The value of obtaining a professional opinion before buying a new boat is underscored by recent unhappy experiences with some boats built outside the United States. A group of boats—both powerboats and sailboats—being imported at this writing have fiberglass hulls with wood decks and deckhouses that have developed rot after just one or two years of use. Even though the decks and houses are covered with a fiberglass sheathing, this rot has originated from water entering around various items of hardware, or from the wood's being wet when the boat was assembled. This is certainly an experience that no one wants, and it can be avoided by seeking experienced assistance. The phrase *caveat emptor*—let the buyer beware—applies very well to the boating industry.

The Surveyor As an Information Source

The tremendous increase in the popularity of boating has favored the growth of allied businesses, including the written information available in magazines and other publications. Generally, the monthly magazines have been doing an excellent job, but a flood of "information" from other sources can only be described as misinformation. For example, a recent newspaper article on the popularity of sailboats, originating from a national news service, stated that "fiberglass and aluminum, the preferred modern materials, are even better suited to sailboat design than for powerboats." Further, "modern sailboats of all sizes are relatively maintenance free as compared with power yachts."

Of course, both of these statements are completely false, as most boat owners already know, but the danger is that inexperienced and first-time owners may believe anything they read. When they do discover the truth, they become disillusioned with the boating industry. The point is that a detached professional such as a naval architect or surveyor should be consulted when a serious boating decision is about to be made.

Probably the best source of written information on modern boats is the periodical magazines, which perform an important function in keeping the public informed of the developments and pitfalls in the industry. The boat owner who takes his cruising safely and seriously would do well to read as many of them as possible. Most people who own boats become very knowledgeable and learn to recognize what is proper and improper about hulls and equipment. Nevertheless, it is always wise to consult a surveyor when considering a purchase.

An example of nonprofessional versus professional opinions arose recently at a boat show exhibit of a new, expensive, fast powerboat whose hull displayed concave dents just where the cradle supports rested against the fiberglass shell. Many experienced owners agreed that if ever there was a boat that needed additional framing, this was it! But the surveyor could tell whether the problem was a local lack of stiffening, or whether the entire hull was too flexible. One obvious defect may or may not condemn an entire hull, depending on the extent of the repairs required to bring the boat to an acceptable condition, whether it is new or used.

The Surveyor's Comments

When the surveyor reports that a particular item on a boat has deteriorated and will require replacement in the near future, he does not mean that it can be neglected until the next time it is convenient to have the boat hauled. It is definitely the responsibility of the boat owner to have each item repaired or replaced as required by the survey report. Examples of such defects would be the erosion of a main engine exhaust elbow or the rusting of the water trap type of muffler in the exhaust line. These deteriorated pieces of equipment may last for a year, or they may leak tomorrow, but they should be replaced just as soon as a problem is discovered. Repair is especially important with exhaust line fittings; we all know the danger of carbon monoxide in exhaust fumes and we understand what can happen in the confined spaces of a boat.

The surveyor often is asked to estimate the remaining life of a faulty piece of equipment—to say approximately when an item will require replacement or under what conditions will it fail. Of course, these are questions that no one can answer, and the surveyor can only reply that the repairs should be made immediately. I once found a badly corroded aluminum mast in an unpainted, rusting steel mast step and recommended immediate repair of the mast and replacement of the step. But the prospective buyer wanted to sail the boat to his home port and have the work done by his local boatyard, so he asked whether I thought the mast would last for the trip. Having no magical powers of prediction, I of course replied in the negative, which was the only safe answer for any surveyor. It could be argued that the mast compression load increases with wind strength and resulting angle of heel, and that the mast should be adequate in winds of less than twelve knots, or fifteen knots, or whatever. But this would only be a theoretical estimate, and certainly not a safe conclusion for a person who wants to go to sea in a sailboat.

During another survey of a sailboat with wood spars, I found rotten wood on the tops of the spreaders; rot had also started inside the masthead sheave boxes in the mizzenmast and mainmast. Such rot is common when sunlight deteriorates the paint or varnish and rainwater seeps into the wood grain. Once again, the prospective purchaser asked whether the boat could be safely used before repairs were made, and the only reasonable answer was that it should not be sailed, as the spreaders could collapse at any time.

The surveyor realizes that he must be ethical in all his statements and actions, but at the same time he wants to be as helpful as he can to the broker, seller, and buyer, as all these people are potential sources of future business. Therefore, he must be diligent in looking for problems and in reporting all the deficiencies he finds, as faults will surely become evident to the new owner in a few months if the survey report does not mention them.

At the same time, however, the surveyor does not want to offend the present owner by condemning the boat just because of a few minor cosmetic problems. The surveyor is really walking a tightrope in most of his work, and he should be careful to confine his remarks to specific facts that can be substantiated. He should avoid generalized statements that can be used to support debatable conclusions.

After the surveyor has submitted his report, the prospective buyer may ask him to estimate the cost of repairs and replacement for all the items mentioned on the report. Quite naturally, the surveyor cannot estimate boatyard labor charges, and he should decline to provide any such cost figures. Often, the buyer just wants a cost total to use as possible leverage in persuading the seller to lower his price. Obviously, the surveyor would do well to steer clear of any such negotiations between buyer and seller. Many times the buyer will also ask the surveyor for an estimate of the boat's value for purpose of obtaining a bank loan or insurance coverage. Such an appraisal may or may not be within the surveyor's experience. Usually the boat broker or insurance agent would be a better judge of price—if he has personal experience with that particular type of boat.

In the last analysis, the surveyor is neither omniscient nor infallible, but he is trained to examine a boat thoroughly and impartially, and he has a store of knowledge that can be drawn on by the owner or prospective owner in order to make wise decisions regarding repair and/or purchase.

CHAPTER 2

The Fiberglass Materials

It has been thirty years since the first boats were built from glass fiber laminates, and these early hulls are still giving good service. Because of its longevity, fiberglass has been very well accepted throughout the world—primarily for large-volume manufacturing, but also for one-of-a-kind, custom hulls.

Fiberglass Compared with Other Materials

When compared with other materials over the lifespan of the hull, fiberglass competes favorably in terms of four primary qualities: strength consistent with light weight, resistance to corrosion, reasonable initial cost, and reasonable cost of maintenance.

1. *Strength Consistent with Light Weight.* Since many ocean-going boats have been built of wood, fiberglass, aluminum, and steel, one must conclude that, given quality construction, all these popular boatbuilding materials provide sufficient strength. When weight is considered, the aluminum hull is normally the lightest for a given structural strength. Wood and glass hulls are about equal in weight in sizes below forty-five feet, but above that, wood construction usually becomes much heavier. Steel hulls are normally heavier for equal stiffness and strength when compared with other materials in boats less than sixty feet in length, but steel is the universal material found in every port in the world, and it is favored for larger boats.

When considering the properties of a boatbuilding material, a designer is most concerned with its stiffness. Hulls should be relatively inflexible, as excessive flexing can cause cracking of the shell. If fiberglass has one disadvantage as a boatbuilding material, it is flexibility. This drawback can be controlled and corrected in construction, however, by installation of framing and by proper bonding of interior joinerwork and bulkheads. These construction details will be explained later.

Before proceeding further, it may be well to define the term *laminate* as used in boat construction. Lamination is simply the placement or bonding of one layer of material on top of another layer of a different material to form a thicker, composite product. In the case of fiberglass laminate, the manufactured product can be a flat sheet or one that is curved to almost any desired shape. Boat hulls, automobile bodies, chair backs, sinks, and tubs are made by a similar process from such laminates. The two materials used in our particular application are a flexible sheet of glass fiber and a liquid chemical called resin, both of which will be described later.

Two other terms that will be used extensively throughout the book are *bonding* and *overlaying*, which have the same meaning in fiberglass boat construction. Bonding or overlaying is the attachment of a fiberglass or wood part to the fiberglass hull. When the edge of a plywood bulkhead, a countertop, a berth, or framing meets the hull, it is secured with long strips of twelve-inch-wide glass fiber material that has been saturated with the liquid resin. The glass material extends about six inches over the hull and the part to be attached. Overlaying is also used to install engine beds and to attach the deck to the hull. Figure 1 (page 26) shows overlaying at the deck-to-hull joint, the attachment of the glass longitudinal stiffeners, and the chainplate knees.

2. *Resistance to Corrosion.* Wood boats are subject to deterioration from rot and marine borers, and great care must be taken to keep fresh water away from both the inside and the outside of the hull. Aluminum hulls of the correct alloy do not corrode from seawater but are subject to galvanic corrosion (electrolysis) and must be carefully monitored when at the dock where shore power is used. Steel hulls must be protected from both galvanic corrosion and rusting, both inside and out.

Fortunately, fiberglass hulls have none of these problems and thus last longer. Although glass laminates will lose their strength if water is allowed to enter the edge of the laminate (at the deck-to-hull joint, for example, or at a through-hull fitting), reasonable care during construction makes this problem almost nonexistent.

3. *Initial Cost.* The construction of a wood, steel, or aluminum hull involves covering frames with plating or planking after the frames have been cut and carefully aligned on the keel structure. This process must be repeated for each hull, and labor is not reduced in volume production. The decreased labor possible in mass production is the primary reason fiberglass hulls are so prevalent in boat manufacturing. True, the cost of permanent molds for fiberglass hulls and decks is substantial, but these costs are defrayed over many hulls, and the subsequent unit cost remains substantially lower than the cost with other materials.

In the case of a custom hull, the selection of a material is really a matter of personal preference, as the initial costs are quite comparable. Steel construction is probably the least expensive, while the cost of aluminum has recently approached three times that of steel. Ferrocement is almost out of the question, as both commercial and amateur builders have found that it requires excessive man-hours, even though the material cost is very low and the resulting hulls are quite durable.

If you are considering a custom boat, you should remember that a boat builder probably is particularly experienced with one material and thus favors it over others for his own construction techniques. Either select a builder first and accommodate your design to his skills, or find a builder who specializes in the material you have chosen. But don't ask a builder to use an unfamiliar material!

A custom fiberglass hull is usually molded ("laid up" or laminated) over a wood plug (a male mold), after which the rough exterior hull surface must be carefully sanded to produce a smooth, fair finish. This sanding and the cost of the disposable plug make a custom glass hull much more expensive than a mass-produced hull, which is made in a highly polished female mold that is used for a large number of

19

hulls. Material costs for a custom glass hull are about halfway between those of steel and aluminum.

4. *Cost of Maintenance.*   No matter how much a person enjoys boating, he will always complain about the high cost of maintenance. This cost, including dockage fees, has probably become the most important factor in the decision whether to purchase a boat and what size boat to buy. In maintenance cost, fiberglass hulls have a decided advantage, especially considering how few hours each year the average pleasure boat is used. Maintenance on a glass hull consists primarily of waxing the exterior to prevent deterioration from the ultraviolet radiation in sunlight, just as you would wax the finish of a fine automobile. Of course, the antifouling bottom paint must be replaced—but that is true of every boat.

Aluminum and steel boats require careful inspection to detect indications of galvanic corrosion, which can lead to expensive repairs, and steel hulls have to be thoroughly coated against rust. Wood construction produces a beautiful, traditional hull, but the high cost of maintenance is turning boat owners to other materials. The seams on planked hulls always seem to require attention, as they move slightly with the loading on the hull, and the seam compound always appears to be shrinking or swelling. Maintenance is never to be taken lightly!

The Fiberglass Laminate

As mentioned before, the glass-reinforced plastic or fiberglass laminate consists of two basic components, the flexible reinforcing glass material and the liquid resin in which it is embedded. These two materials are chemically bonded to form a solid, rigid sheet. By the addition of subsequent layers, they can be laminated to any desired thickness.

The Glass Fibers.   The first component, the reinforcing glass material, consists of very thin strands bundled together in long fibers. These fibers are then used to manufacture three basic forms of flexible sheet material—cloth, mat, and woven roving. When you look at a cross section of a finished boat hull laminate, you will normally not be able to tell what type of glass material has been used unless you are very experienced with laminates, but each has its own characteristics and applications.

Cloth is a finely woven material with a satiny finish that looks like any shiny, heavy white cloth. Because many plies are required to build up the desired thickness for a hull, cloth is more expensive than mat or woven roving, and the latter materials are used in alternate layers to form the primary laminate in most boat hull applications. Cloth can be ordered in weights from 6 to 12 ounces per square yard. It is normally used only as a final ply inside the laminate so the interior hull surface will be smooth. However, laminated cloth has excellent strength properties and it conforms easily to compound curvatures, so it may be found in intricate structural parts such as engine beds and sailboat chainplate knees.

Glass mat consists of randomly arranged fibers about four to eight inches in length, bonded together with resin to form a sheet without much initial strength. In fact, mat can be pulled apart easily with the hands, as it is not woven like cloth or woven roving. The weight of the mat, curiously, is designated in ounces per square foot rather than ounces per square yard like the other materials, and is available in weights of ¾ to 3 ounces per square foot. Initially, the inside of the mold for a production boat is sprayed with a gel coat of the outside hull color, followed by two layers of ¾-ounce mat. This fine mat is used to insure that no voids (air bubbles) are left behind the gel coat and to prevent the coarse weave of the woven roving from showing through (a defect called pattern transfer). After that, most boat builders use 1½-ounce mat and 18-ounce woven roving for the bulk of the hull.

Woven roving is a very heavy weave of glass fiber bundles that looks like thick, white burlap and is usually available in weights from 14 to 32 ounces per square yard. Also available is a material called *unidirectional woven roving*, which is manufactured with a greater number of strands of glass fiber in one direction than the other. Unidirectional woven roving can be used as local reinforcement in areas of high stress in one direction, such as at chainplates, but it must be oriented so that the greatest number of glass fibers lie in the direction of the highest load. To avoid possible errors, most boat builders do not use this product, but prefer to apply extra plies of mat and woven roving as required. (Using fewer kinds of material also simplifies purchasing and inventory for the builder and helps insure a rapid turnover of supplies. Glass material should not be allowed to sit in a humid atmosphere before laminating, as it will absorb moisture and its resultant strength will be decreased.)

The Resins. The liquid resins used for the "plastic" part of the laminate can be either polyester or epoxy formulations, but polyester is universally used because of its lower cost—about one-fourth that of epoxy. Epoxy resins have greater adhesive properties than polyesters, however, and are thus preferred for repairs to damaged hulls. Epoxies are also important for attaching a cured glass laminate to another laminate (secondary bonding), but care must be taken on vertical surfaces, as the resin becomes thin during hardening and may drain away from the glass, leaving a laminate that is unsaturated and weak.

The polyester resins are mixed with a small amount of liquid called *hardener*, which starts the chemical process of solidifying the resin. The amount of hardener is carefully controlled to allow about twenty minutes of working time before the resin becomes too thick to use. In this time, the laminating crew must carefully saturate the glass material with the resin, using a brush or spray gun. They must be careful, however, not to use excessive resin, which will result in a laminate of lower strength. To insure complete saturation with a minimum of resin, workers roll the glass into the mold, one layer at a time, using plastic rollers that are not chemically affected by the resin. As the resin initially hardens, it gives off considerable heat, and the mold must be firmly braced and stiffened to prevent warping. Since resins are thermosetting, they cannot be softened by applying heat after the molding process.

All resins should be kept free of contaminants and should be mixed with other chemicals, additives, or thinners only in accordance with the manufacturer's instructions.

If a fire occurs aboard a boat with a glass hull, the resin in the laminate will burn unless the manufacturer used an additive to make the finished product fire-resistant. You cannot determine visually whether this additive is present, so the surveyor and owner must rely on information from the builder, who purchases resin with the proper chemical formulation. As an alternative, the interior of the hull could be coated with a fire-retardant paint—if it has not already been coated with a decorative finish.

Core Materials

As mentioned earlier, glass hulls usually require supplementary stiffening. Part of it is supplied by overlaying the edges of bulkheads, countertops, berths, and other joinerwork to the glass hull on both sides with twelve-inch-wide strips of alternate layers of glass mat, resin, and woven roving. If the inside of the hull surface is clean and well sanded, a good bond will result and the hull will be adequately stiffened if these overlaid members are close enough together.

However, under the berths and settees the unstiffened area becomes excessive, and framing or stiffeners must be added. Such framing involves the installation of nonstructural half-round or rectangular forms overlaid with three plies of 1½-ounce mat alternating with three plies of 18-ounce woven roving. These stiffeners can be located either transversely or longitudinally, from twelve to twenty inches apart, depending on the designed hull thickness.

Framing of this kind requires careful workmanship and considerable man-hours and adds to the weight of the hull. For these reasons (particularly pursuit of lighter weight), some builders prefer to construct their hulls with a *core material* sandwiched between two layers of glass fiber laminate (see Figure 1). The use of core construction provides a stiffened laminate of somewhat lighter weight than a solid laminate and is thus desirable for special purposes such as racing hulls. Normally, core construction is more expensive, simply because of the cost of the core material, but it has the advantage of providing good sound and heat insulation.

9.2 A   L.O.A. 29'-11"

Thirty-foot production fiberglass sailboat with hull and rig designed by the author. (Photo courtesy S 2 Yachts, Inc., Holland, Michigan 49423.)

Most core materials have sufficient compressive strength to withstand relatively light loads such as the crew working on deck, but they may fail where high, concentrated loads are involved. In these areas, such as at through-hull fittings and at keel bolts, the core should be replaced with a solid laminate, and the laminate itself should normally be increased in thickness in the general area of such hull penetrations.

Through-hull fittings—pieces of hardware that project through holes in the hull—include speedometer indicators, fathometer transducers, sink drains, cockpit scupper drains, and seacocks for the engine cooling water intake and toilet intake and discharge. In sandwich construction, if a through-hull fitting were tightened to make a watertight seal, the internal core material would be squeezed until it separated from the top and bottom fiberglass facings. Thus a solid laminate or a watertight fiberglass pipe bushing should be employed at these penetrations. Because boats may have quite a few through-hull fittings, it becomes impractical to install a core material below the waterline, except in very large custom hulls. The decision to use a core is based largely on personal preference and budget; the cost of a bare hull is only about 16 percent of the cost of a completed boat.

Although builders may have divided opinions about the use of core construction in hulls, most agree that all *decks*—at least for recreational boats—should be built with a fiberglass core sandwich. This eliminates the need for supporting deck beams in most hulls under forty feet in length, thus providing another two inches of headroom inside the hull.

Materials used as sandwich cores include balsa wood (cut so that the edge grain faces the two laminates), plastic foams, plywood, and other proprietary materials. Most of these cores perform very well, but each has its specific applications and the manufacturer's instructions should be followed carefully. The boat owner and surveyor would do well to rely on the experience of the boat builder when investigating core materials.

Sandwich core construction techniques can be employed in special applications that utilize the excellent properties of light weight and

25

FIGURE 1
Core Materials in the Deck and for Longitudinal Stiffeners

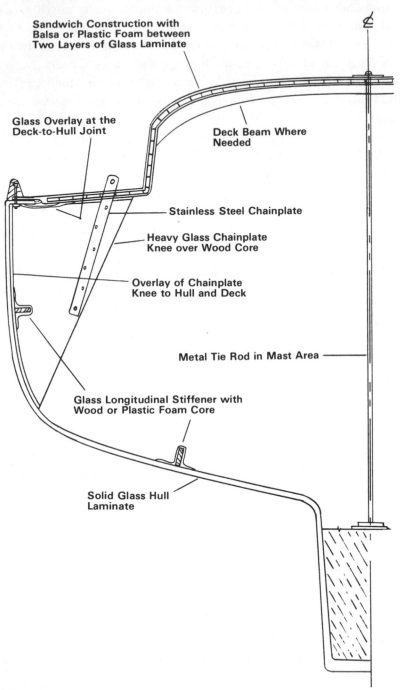

Sandwich Construction with
Balsa or Plastic Foam between
Two Layers of Glass Laminate

Glass Overlay at the
Deck-to-Hull Joint

Deck Beam Where
Needed

Stainless Steel Chainplate

Heavy Glass Chainplate
Knee over Wood Core

Overlay of Chainplate
Knee to Hull and Deck

Metal Tie Rod in Mast Area

Glass Longitudinal Stiffener with
Wood or Plastic Foam Core

Solid Glass Hull
Laminate

26

stiffness to good advantage. For example, multiple layers of glass laminate and core can be fabricated to achieve almost any desired thickness in any shape. I have successfully used this construction method to support the compressive load of a sailboat mizzenmast and to spread the load throughout the molded fiberglass deck structure. The total sandwich thickness was over three inches, and it was built up in a mounded or humped shape on the cabin top so that headroom would not be reduced inside the hull. The resulting bulge on the cabin top was faired into a sliding hatch cover so that the overall shape was not obtrusive. However, I would not recommend this procedure for the much higher compressive loads of a sailboat mainmast. The alternative to this sandwich mast support construction was to put a post under the mast, but this would have ruined the walking space inside the boat. This sandwich construction technique has also been used to stiffen the deck and distribute the loading under boat davits and under sailboat mainsheet travelers.

Some fiberglass boats are built with inside frames, longitudinals, floor timbers, and deck beams of wood or metal attached to the hull as structural reinforcement. Use of such members is called *composite construction* and is not recommended. Composite construction depends on a chemical resin bond or mechanical bolting for success. It is not to be confused with a nonstructural application in which a wood or plastic foam core serves only as a form over which glass is laminated to create longitudinal stringers, deck beams, or other framing. In this latter situation, only the glass overlay to the hull bears the load, and the inside core could be removed (if it were possible) after the glass has cured. In fact, some structural framing for glass hulls is prefabricated separately with no core and is afterward bonded to the hull with wide strips of mat and woven roving.

Composite construction is suspect because it is very difficult to bond glass to steel or aluminum; the metal is not porous and will not absorb the resin. Wood will bond to glass fairly well except when the wood is oily or still contains sap. Also, the properties of wood are different from those of glass and continued, minute flexing of the hull will loosen the bond between wood and glass if there is a high degree of loading on that particular area. The only sure way to attach a different material, especially metals, to a glass laminate is by through-bolting. Cleats, engine mountings, and propeller shaft struts should be through-bolted, and if an aluminum pipe is used as a post supporting the deck, it too should be through-bolted and not just overlaid with glass to the underside of the deck. The same reasoning applies to any metals attached to fiberglass, but ideally the reinforcing material should usually be glass. In other applications, it is strongly recommended that glass laminate be used to form framing, stiffeners, brackets, and bracing, as nothing bonds to a glass laminate like more glass.

An understanding of the fiberglass laminate and its components—glass fiber and resin—give the boat owner and the surveyor a basis for evaluating the construction and integrity of a glass hull, the installation of its through-hull fittings, and the significance of any cracks, blisters, or damage. In the next chapter, we will examine the design of the laminate and framing.

CHAPTER 3

Design of the Laminate and Framing

When a fiberglass hull is designed, the thickness of the laminate and the spacing of the framing must be considered simultaneously. The designer must be concerned with the size of unsupported panels of hull surface. Thus, each small area of surface must be considered to be sure that it will withstand the expected stress and that the calculated deflection or bending of the unsupported panel is within design limits.

If the hull does not meet allowable stress requirements, or if calculated deflection is greater than it should be, additional stiffeners (framing) must be added, or the thickness of the laminate must be increased, or both. Of course, the correct size and thickness of the stiffeners must be calculated as well.

The calculations for thickness and deflection are based on the properties of a one-inch strip of laminate across the panel; it is assumed that this strip acts as a uniformly loaded beam. A comprehensive discussion of these calculations, along with examples for both displacement speed and planing boats is presented in the book *Fiberglass Boat Design and Construction* by Robert J. Scott (Clinton Corners, N.Y.: John de Graff, Inc., 1973).

The importance of framing and longitudinal stiffeners cannot be overemphasized. For example, in an average small powerboat with longitudinal stiffeners spaced 20 inches apart, the required laminate thickness is about 0.34 inch. If the stiffeners were spaced 40 inches apart, the hull thickness would have to be 0.70 inch! This difference in required hull bottom thickness amounts to 2.88 pounds per square foot and would result in a very expensive increase in hull costs, to say nothing of the loss in performance caused by increased weight. We can conclude, therefore, that it is much less expensive for the manufacturer to achieve stiffness by installing closely spaced framing rather than by increasing hull thickness.

In addition to determining the necessary overall thickness and framing requirements of the hull and deck, the local loads on each must be carefully investigated. A planing powerboat receives a considerable impact loading on the bow sections when it slams into a wave, and these areas must be well stiffened. Just try to sleep on the forward V-berths when the boat is underway if you have any doubts about impact loads!

Surprisingly enough, a sailboat, although its speed is much slower, is subject to the same impact loading when sailing to windward in seas over three feet in height. Because of the high weights of the mast and rigging and the high center of driving force, the sailboat pitches considerably when sailing into a head sea, and when the downward motion of the bow hits the crest of a wave, the high impact loading greatly reduces the speed of the boat. Once again, trying to sleep on the forward berths will prove the point.

There is just no substitute for framing and longitudinal stiffeners in the bow area. Of course, the frequency of the impact loading over a period of time determines whether or not the material is in danger of being stressed to the point of failure. The boat should always be designed to withstand the highest stresses that may be encountered over the lifetime of the hull.

Local reinforcement of the basic laminate is necessary in areas of high stress such as propeller shaft struts (bearings), propeller shaft logs, rudder posts, sailboat chainplates, and the bottoms of keels. The hull is subject to the highest local loading when it is pounding against a dock, aground on a rock, or hauled and sitting on blocks. For example, the designer must assume that the entire weight of the boat is resting on two blocks one foot in length when the boat is dry-docked. The surveyor should be particularly observant in these areas to see whether the keel laminate is being crushed, as the side braces usually do nothing more than keep the boat from tipping.

30

In a powerboat, not only the bow sections but also the aft half of the bottom deserves careful attention in design and construction. There, the lack of stiffeners or a thin laminate shell will result in a bottom structure that is too flexible, and the laminate will flex in different directions in different areas such as around shaft struts and logs. When this happens, the propeller shaft comes out of alignment with the engine and strut bearings, and excessive wear will quickly ruin the bearings and shaft log (stuffing box). The engine beds not only provide a place to bolt the engines securely but serve to transmit the loads and vibration stresses. These beds must be as long as possible and must be braced transversely with fiberglass webs to the hull (see Figure 3).

When designing the hull laminate and structure, the total weight of the glass must be carefully calculated to insure that the boat will float correctly on the designed waterline when all other parts and equipment are installed. The lower part of Figure 2 will assist in this procedure, as it shows the weight of bare glass hulls as they are removed from the mold. It will also assist in comparing one hull with another. The reason for the lighter weight of sailboat hulls of the same waterline length is that they usually have less freeboard than powerboats and the bow and stern of a sailboat, particularly the stern, are much finer and narrower. These bare hull weights are averages that have been obtained from calculations and from actual weighing of hulls by various manufacturers.

The upper part of Figure 2 is a curve showing the average weight of boats when fully loaded in operating condition. Wide variations in displacement will occur, depending on the installed equipment and type of hull construction. The advertised displacements that appear in manufacturers' brochures are sometimes misleading, as they could be full-load weights or the weight of the light boat as it is delivered from the factory, without fuel, water, crew, galley stores, clothes, and personal gear.

Manufacturers have varying techniques of construction, but the surveyor or owner should concentrate on the two major points of concern—the laminate thickness and the spacing of the framing. Figure 3 shows the typical construction of a small fiberglass powerboat

FIGURE 2
WEIGHTS OF A BARE HULL AND OF A COMPLETED BOAT

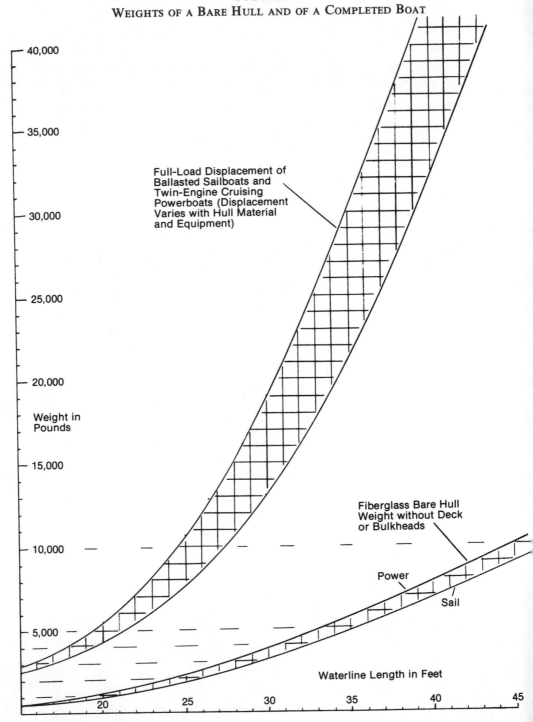

FIGURE 3
TYPICAL CONSTRUCTION OF A FIBERGLASS POWERBOAT HULL UNDER THIRTY FEET IN LENGTH

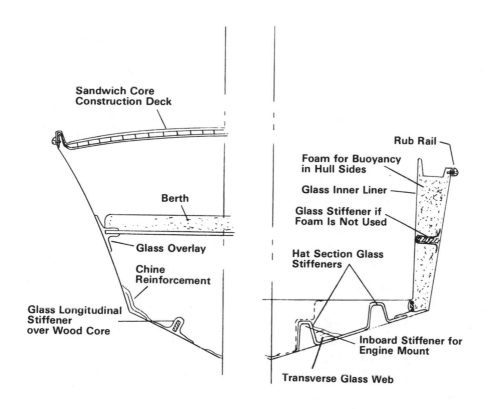

with stiffeners installed in several different ways. The forward berth is normally made of plywood and is overlaid with glass to the side of the hull both above and below the wood. This overlay consists of two or three plies of alternating 1½-ounce mat and 18-ounce woven roving, applied to the hull surface after it has been sanded with a coarse grit. Thus, the plywood berth forms a good stiffener.

As noted earlier, all wood joinerwork should be overlaid in a similar manner, wherever the edge of the wood butts against the hull. In the bottom, forward (at the left in Figure 3), a nonstructural wood core is overlaid with glass laminate to form an effective longitudinal stiffener. However, the *ends* of the stiffener also must be glassed to bulkheads, both forward and aft. Or, if this longitudinal stiffener butts against the curving bow section of the hull, instead of against a bulkhead, the load produced by the end of the stiffener must be distributed so that a hard spot will not result. Thus, the end of the stiffener should rest on a pad of two alternating plies of glass laminate, about one foot square. This same procedure should be used where a transverse member, such as a floor beam, butts against the side of the hull (see Figure 4).

It should be noted that the deck shown in Figure 3 is of core construction, so the deck will not flex when walked upon. The core material stops just short of the sheer (the intersection of deck and hull). The deck and hull, with the rub rail, are bolted together in this area. Very high loads occur at this point, especially when the boat hits a dock or piling, and any core material would be crushed and delaminated over a period of time. After this deck-to-hull joint has been bolted, the area inside the joint should be overlaid with three alternating layers of glass mat and woven roving.

In the aft section of the boat (at the right in Figure 3), a fiberglass inner liner forms the cockpit sole and sides. Seats also can be molded in. This inner liner must be well supported, as shown, with stiffeners that also prevent flexing of the hull. In no case can the inner liner be allowed to flex independently of the hull. Both require stiffening and they should be bonded together, with glass or with intermediate framing, wherever the two skins are close together.

Figure 4 shows the typical construction of a fiberglass sailboat,

34

FIGURE 4
TYPICAL CONSTRUCTION OF A FIBERGLASS SAILBOAT USING A GLASS INNER LINER

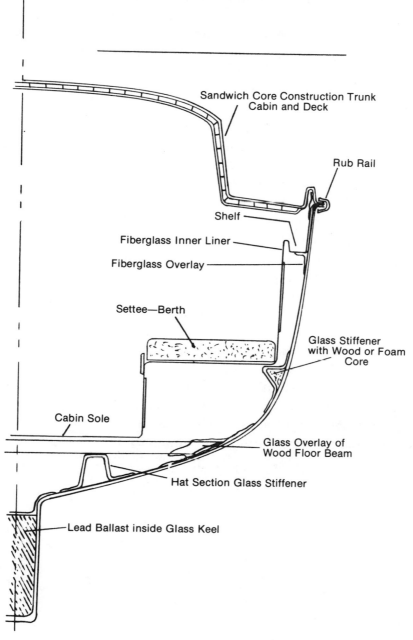

Sandwich Core Construction Trunk Cabin and Deck

Rub Rail

Shelf

Fiberglass Inner Liner

Fiberglass Overlay

Settee—Berth

Glass Stiffener with Wood or Foam Core

Cabin Sole

Glass Overlay of Wood Floor Beam

Hat Section Glass Stiffener

Lead Ballast inside Glass Keel

with a glass inner liner forming the settee-berth and the cabin sole. This liner extends up to the sheer and covers the rough interior of the hull. Such a liner looks very good, but it makes it impossible for the surveyor or owner to inspect the hull surface, except where the liner is cut out for lockers or drawers. The hull must be adequately stiffened before the liner is installed, and the stiffeners can serve to support the liner, too.

The construction of a sailboat is very similar to that of a power-boat, with the exception of the rigging and keel, and the requirements for sound laminate reinforcement apply to both types of hull. The keel of a sailboat can be constructed in one of three ways: (1) the hull can be molded without a keel, and the keel bolted to the hull later; (2) the hull can be molded with a shallow keel, to which external ballast is bolted; or (3) the hull can be constructed with a fully molded glass keel designed to receive internal ballast. The last alternative is shown in Figure 4. The keel has been constructed as part of the hull, and lead ballast is inside. This arrangement is the least costly and probably produces fewer maintenance problems than the others. The lead ballast can be cast in one piece, or it can consist of lead shot bound together with polyester resin.

To sum up, the laminate and framing together must provide adequate strength to support expected stresses and loads on the hull. Although the exact calculations of strength versus weight and accommodation space are the job of the designer, the surveyor and the knowledgeable boat owner should understand the importance of hull stiffness and the ways it can be accomplished.

CHAPTER 4

Construction Details

Boat owners who have never seen boats in production may not be able to visualize how a hull is molded. It is difficult to imagine that flexible, cloth-like materials such as mat and woven roving can be made into a smooth, hard surface the size of a hull.

This chapter, therefore, outlines details of construction. The text has a dual purpose: It clarifies manufacturing procedures for readers who are unfamiliar with them, and it emphasizes points of construction that concern the surveyor of the finished craft.

One-Off Construction

First, let's examine one-off or custom fabrication and the methods used when only one or two hulls are going to be made from a mold.

It is normally too expensive to build a cavity (or female) mold if just a few hulls are to be taken from it. Instead, one-off construction begins with a rough, expendable "plug" that looks just like a wood boat before it is planked. The wood frames of the plug are connected with longitudinal stringers spaced about four inches apart, and the entire plug is covered with a sheet of plastic to prevent the resin (which will go on the outside) from sticking to the wood. In some cases, the builder prefers to plank the hull partially with very thin sheets of wood, called *veneers*.

The fiberglass laminate is built up on this plug to the desired thickness, using great care with each ply so that the resulting surface is a fair and smooth curve. The application sequence of the glass plies must be planned carefully before lamination is begun, since the designed hull thickness varies in different areas. Furthermore, the glass

Wood plug for a custom, one-of-a-kind glass hull before lamination of the fiberglass.

Finished glass hull for a custom 38-foot centerboard ketch.

material comes in four-foot widths that must be overlapped at the edges, creating thicker areas. Layers of glass and resin are built up over the mold.

When the glass is completely laid up, its exterior surface is rough and usually shows some high spots and general lack of fairness. As a result, many hours are spent filling the low areas with a mixture of glass microballoons (small glass beads) and resin. Then the entire hull is painstakingly sanded to achieve a perfectly smooth finish. After application of priming coats, the hull is painted with a polyester gel coat, epoxy, or polyurethane paint.

Volume Molding Methods

When a large number of identical hulls will be made, a glass cavity mold is prepared. First, a wood plug is constructed, and then the cavity mold is taken from the plug. This plug may be a finished custom glass hull, a wood hull, or a hull built of some other material. A perfect finish is rubbed onto the outside of the plug, then it is waxed and a gel coat is sprayed on, followed by many layers of glass laminate. The glass is built up to form a mold at least five-eighths inch thick. The mold is then reinforced on the outside with steel or aluminum pipe welded into a solid framework so that the mold will retain its shape after many hulls have been removed from it.

After the mold is removed from the plug, many more hours are required to rub and wax the inside (where the hulls will be laid up) to produce a high gloss. After it is smooth and waxed, the mold is sprayed with a releasing agent and the color gel coat for the first hull. The laminations are then started, one layer after another. Preparing the mold after construction and laminating a hull require about five days for a forty-foot boat, in comparison with ten weeks for a custom hull.

Combining glass material and resin in a mold this way is known as the *contact*, or *hand layup*, method of molding; the laminate is cured without application of pressure from an outside source. This contact molding is almost universally employed in boat manufacturing, although other, more sophisticated techniques are available for the very high-volume production of small boats.

Interior of the bow section of a fiberglass powerboat mold, showing where an addition has been made to the height of the sheer. Also visible are spots that have been repaired after a hull had stuck to the mold.

Exterior of a fiberglass powerboat mold with spray equipment for use with resins and gel coats in the foreground.

When the hand layup lamination is completed, it results in a glass structure with a weight of approximately ninety-six pounds per cubic foot. Thus, a piece one-half inch thick and one foot square would weigh four pounds. Of this, approximately 30 percent would be glass material. This is an average value found in actual practice, and it conceivably could vary by 5 percent, depending on the skill and quality control of the laminator. Most builders have the glass precut and the resin carefully measured for a particular hull prior to laminating to insure that excessive resin will not be poured into the laminate. Usually the finished hulls are weighed as they are removed from the mold, providing a good measure of quality control.

Generally, a laminate of alternating plies of 1½-ounce per square foot mat and 18-ounce woven roving will produce a thickness of 0.09 inch per pair (0.05 inch for the mat and 0.04 inch for the woven roving). The gel coat is about 0.015 inch thick and each layer of ¾-ounce mat next to it is about 0.025 inch in thickness.

With a normal laminate, as described above, it is common to achieve a flexural strength of 29,000 psi (pounds per square inch), a tensile strength of about 14,800 psi, and a compressive strength of approximately 22,500 psi. These values vary widely with the amount of glass in the laminate, and also require the use of a safety factor between 1.5 and 4.0, depending on the application.

Some boats have been made successfully with a laminate composed entirely of mat and resin, without any woven roving. Mat and resin alone result in much lower strength properties and can be used only if the laminate is thicker than normal and if framing is closely spaced. Some small modern boats have been made with an all-mat layup without benefit of framing, and there have been failures of these hulls.

An all-mat laminate is used in the manufacture of nonstructural parts for industries other than boating. In this production method a special spray gun (chopper gun) simultaneously deposits resin and short glass strands in the mold. This procedure saves a great deal of time and lowers the production costs in applications for which it is intended. This method should not, however, be used in boat hull molds without a careful engineering analysis of the structure.

Fiberglass molded laminates have very good physical properties for use in many applications. Specific data can be obtained from the Owens-Corning Fiberglas Corporation, Industrial Materials Division, Toledo, Ohio 43601. They have been most helpful to me and to others in the boating industry.

The Deck and Cabin

The hull mold is normally a large, smooth open area. It is relatively uncomplicated to build when compared with the deck-cabin-and-cockpit mold—also generally a one-piece molding. (Exceptions to a single-piece molding sometimes occur for designs having reverse curves and special shapes, but it is difficult to join two molded glass pieces together with a neat-looking seam, so most builders try to have a single mold.)

Because a deck mold is so complex, the builder must take great care in preparation to insure that each surface has sufficient slope, or draft, to allow the finished piece to be released from the mold with ease. In addition, each corner and hard-to-reach area must have a large radius—that is, it must be free of sharp angles—so that the laminating crew can easily work out the air bubbles next to the gel coat and push the layers of glass into a sufficiently saturated laminate.

Fortunately, this requirement for a large radius has a second benefit—it helps prevent a concentration of stress, which can occur at a sharp corner, a hole, or a spot where a stiffener ends abruptly. The corners of a hatch opening and the edges of the cabin side both need large radii to prevent future cracking of the surface gel coat. An abrupt change in shape results in a high concentration of stress, and when additional loading is applied, such as pounding into a seaway, the stress level may be excessive for the material and cracks may develop. The first sign of this problem is the appearance of hairline cracks in the exterior gel coat, showing areas that the surveyor should investigate.

The Deck-to-Hull Joint

The attachment of the deck to the hull is one of the most important on the boat, and Figures 3 and 4 show two types of joint configuration. It is generally accepted that the deck and hull laminates should overlap and that they should be bolted together, using a layer of wet mat at the overlap. After bolting, the joint is further bonded with three alternating layers of mat and woven roving on the inside, extending about six inches on either side of the seam. This overlapping of the deck and the hull laminate may be located on the hull side, on the deck just inboard of the sheer, or on the molded glass toerail, as desired. The raw edge of each laminate layer should be sealed with resin to prevent the entry of water, which could start delamination. If water has been entering this deck-to-hull joint, the edge of the laminate will appear discolored and almost black with mildew, and a repair will have to be made by cutting out the water-soaked area and building up new laminate.

Hardware Attachment

Hairline cracks indicating excessive stress can appear in the gel coat around hardware on the deck. All such hardware—cleats, pad-eyes, lifeline stanchions—should be through-bolted to the deck. It is not sufficient, however, simply to put a washer under the nut on the bottom of a bolt. Each piece of hardware should have a wood or aluminum backing plate three-sixteenths or one-quarter inch thick, large enough in area to extend at least one inch outside the bolts. Particular care must be given to any hardware on the side of the cabin, where the laminate may be substantially thinner than the deck. Heavy deck equipment that receives high loads—bowsprits, anchor windlasses, and fishing chairs—requires additional glass, posts, and framing under the deck and extending down to the hull in order to distribute the load adequately. The surveyor should examine the area around all such attached equipment for cracking and other evidence of stress.

The Cabin Top

It is very important to prevent the cabin top as well as the deck from flexing. The cabin is often overlooked, however—particularly if the builder uses a molded fiberglass overhead liner to cover the rough glass on the underside of the roof. (Such a liner is similar to the inner liners shown in Figures 3 and 4.) Too often, the tops of the bulkheads are not secured to the roof, or trunk cabin, allowing the roof to flex upward. It may be hard to visualize the roof moving up and down, but it sometimes happens when the boat rolls hard against the dock or into a steep sea.

This cabin top movement frequently occurs in sailboats, and to prevent it, all wood boats have tie rods installed between the roof and the floor timbers (refer back to Figure 1). These rods are normally half-inch brass, threaded both top and bottom for attachment. The movement occurs when sailing to windward, with the rigging tight on the windward side, exerting a horizontal force on the chainplates and tending to push the sheers together. At the same time, the leeward side of the hull is uniformly supported by the water. The resultant load on the cabin top is upward, in a vertical direction. If the tops of the bulkheads are not glassed to the roof, or if the cabin top has a large open area without partial bulkheads, tie rods should be installed.

As any boat pitches, rolls, and yaws in a seaway, the racking strains placed on the hull and superstructure are applied in different directions, especially to the cabin sides and roof. The cabin sides are particularly vulnerable in a design with a flying bridge and large windows all around. Tie rods and bulkheads secured to the roof are very important in this instance, but they are often neglected in favor of a large, open cabin. An alternative reinforcing procedure requires the installation of deck beams glassed to the underside of the roof and the ends glassed to vertical posts, which are in turn heavily glassed to the cabin sides. The bottoms of these posts should extend down until they intersect and are glassed to the hull. This forms a fairly stiff arch-type structure, and similar arches should be located about four feet apart, throughout the length of the cabin.

Sailboat Rigging

The mast and the wire rope that supports it have been carefully designed by the naval architect. The surveyor's job is normally just to inspect them for corrosion and to see that the fittings that join the parts of the rigging assembly are intact. The rigging on a sailboat is attached to the hull through steel straps called chainplates, which must be strongly secured. The headstay and backstay chainplates are normally bolted through the hull with aluminum backing plates under the nuts and washers. The hull should be reinforced locally in the area of all chainplates with three alternating layers of mat and woven roving at least twelve inches in width.

If the boat has a jibstay in addition to the headstay, it must be secured to the hull with a strap, rod, or wire rope; the load should not bear on the deck alone. Very often, the jibstay is located aft of the headstay just at the forepeak bulkhead, so the load is transmitted through the bulkhead to the hull. If possible, it is good practice to use a bent flat bar as a backing plate for both the jib tack plate and the headstay at the stem. The bar takes the tack plate load off the deck and transfers it to the hull. At this point, it may be well to mention that the mast step and all chainplates should be grounded with No. 8 wire to the keel bolts or to an outside metal ground plate for lightning protection.

The shroud chainplates may be bolted through the hull, but more often they are set inboard from the sheer and bolted to a large plywood-core knee that is heavily glassed to both the deck and the hull (refer back to Figure 1). The wood normally used for this knee is only a nonstructural core. The strength is provided by the glass overlay, which should consist of three layers of alternating mat and woven roving on both sides of the wood, extending at least six inches onto the hull and the underside of the deck. Bedding compound is applied around each chainplate where it passes through the deck laminate, and a cover plate is installed around the chainplate to hold the bedding in place.

Some sailboats have U-shaped bolts fastened through the deck to secure the rigging turnbuckles. The diameter of these bolts should be at least twice that of the wire rope rigging, and they should be of the same material. Under the deck, each U-bolt must be fastened to a heavy knee or steel bracket to transmit the load to the hull. One method is to use a steel angle bracket under each end of the U-bolt;

the bracket in turn is bolted to a knee that is heavily glassed to the hull. Another solution is to use tie rods between the U-bolts and the mast step, but this can usually be accomplished only for the upper shrouds. Alternatively, the underside of the deck could be overlaid to the hull in the area of the U-bolts to a thickness of approximately one-half inch of glass laminate, forming an angle to distribute the load. This latter construction detail is particularly important if highly loaded deck hardware such as windlasses and boat davits is installed. The overlay to the hull should extend about twenty inches down from the sheer, with the same overlap under the deck.

Mast Steps

Some installations, such as sailboat masts stepped on deck, or large winches, place such a high compressive load on the deck laminate that the core material may be crushed. In these cases it is necessary to use a compression tube, usually cut from aluminum pipe, around each bolt. The compression tube is used in addition to load-distributing aluminum backing plates installed both above and below the deck. Thus the loads are transmitted to the supporting structure below the deck (a bulkhead or pipe) by the compression tubes instead of by the sandwich laminate, which doesn't have the strength.

In this discussion of glass laminates for boat hulls, we do not want to stray too far into the details of rigging and equipment, but the construction of a mast step on a motorsailer or sailboat of any type is so critical that it deserves to be included. The treatment here is designed to help the surveyor conduct a proper inspection.

The mainmast compression load on the bottom of the hull varies widely with the height of the rig, the beam, and the stability of the hull, and it can be greater than the weight of the boat itself. For this reason, the load must be widely distributed over an area that is at least eighteen inches by thirty inches on a forty-foot hull. This distribution can be accomplished quite easily in a glass hull by laminating mat and woven roving inside the hull to a thickness that provides the necessary flat surface area.

Usually it is desirable to allow a free flow of bilgewater past the mast step to the bilge pump, and a water duct can be formed by placing a plastic pipe one inch in diameter next to the hull before the mast step flat is laminated. The mast actually sits inside a collar that is welded to a plate, and both collar and plate should be aluminum for a wood or aluminum mast. Drain holes should be drilled around the collar, for rainwater enters the various openings in the mast and will cause oxidation of the bottom of the mast if not allowed to drain away. The bottom of the mast should be painted with the correct paint for the material, or covered with a specially formulated mast coating.

It is disastrous to have an aluminum mast sitting in an unpainted steel mast step or collar. The steel rusts and the aluminum oxidizes, and the two actions seem to promote each other. The parts bond together until the bottom of the mast is completely corroded and has to be cut off and a new, taller mast foundation installed.

The consequences of such a situation were once made vividly evident to me. A sailboat was to be hauled for trailer transportation to another port, and the mast was to be removed first with a crane. The boat was only three months old, but it had an aluminum mast inside an unpainted steel mast step. The rigging was freed and the crane began to lift the mast by a strap under the spreaders. But the crane operator wisely stopped when he found that he was lifting the entire boat out of the water with the mast still in place! On investigation, it was found that corrosion was so advanced that the steel step had to be unbolted from the glass foundation and a large sledgehammer used to disengage the mast from the step. Beware of dissimilar metals!

Very often the mast is located on top of the lead ballast, if the lead is inside the glass hull. The ballast forms a good bearing area for the mast step, which can be secured to the lead with lag screws. For two reasons, it is important to cover the lead with glass laminate overlaid to the hull or to the sides of the keel. First, if the lead ballast and the aluminum mast step are in contact with each other and if water seeps between them, there is a possibility of electrolysis that will corrode the mast step. Second, if water runs between the lead and the inside of the glass keel laminate, it may freeze in the winter and expand sufficiently to cause failure of the laminate. The surveyor should examine the mast step carefully for all these potential problems.

Bulkheads and Stiffeners

Previous mention has been made of the necessity of overlaying both sides of all bulkheads and joinerwork to the hull. *Joinerwork* is a term used to describe a boat's interior cabinetry and furnishings that are handcrafted from wood. In modern practice, usage of the term has expanded to include all the inside assemblies that make the boat more livable and attractive.

Overlaying is especially important at the bottom of a bulkhead, where the wood is acting as transverse framing. This overlay at the bottom must be watertight up to the level of the cabin flooring so that any bilgewater will not soak into the wood. Water would not only loosen the glass from the wood, but would also start delamination of the plywood. As an additional precaution, the edges of the wood should be sealed with resin before installation.

In today's fiberglass boat building industry it is almost a practical necessity to use wood for bulkheads and for forms inside the glass laminate when fabricating engine beds, other longitudinal stiffeners, and transverse framing. Future developments and cost reductions may result in more use of other plastic-faced or aluminum-faced foam sandwich materials, but their much lighter weight is not always an advantage in boat building. As previously emphasized, the attachment of the bulkhead to the glass hull is the key element in the structure, and the material of which the bulkhead is made must be compatible with polyester resin. This compatibility factor is another reason for using wood or plastic and not metal for bulkheads or framing.

Designers of racing sailboats tend to eliminate interior bulkheads to reduce weight, replacing them with aluminum pipes secured to the deck and hull. These pipes are necessary for adequate structural support and should be bolted to the glass with end plates welded to the pipe. Or fiberglass pipe can be easily glassed to the existing shell. The use of metal reinforcement to provide a strong backbone or framing for a fiberglass boat is not necessary, since fiberglass is perfectly

50

capable of withstanding the loads imposed on the hull if it has been properly designed. Also, the metal will react differently from the glass fiber laminate under load, because it has different strength properties and resistance to bending.

Tanks

Fuel and water tanks may be fabricated of metal or glass laminate. If glass is used, however, the tank should be separate from the hull and not integral—that is, the hull should *not* form one side of the tank. Integral tanks are usually fabricated after the hull has been molded, with a secondary bond between the tank and the hull. The builder assumes this bond to be adequate to make a watertight joint, but I do not believe that this is a reasonable assumption, even if excellent workmanship is employed. Subsequent flexing of the hull or banging against a dock may loosen this secondary bond, and the entire contents of the tank will be spilled into the bilges. Fiberglass has served well for both fuel and water tanks, but only if the tanks are separate from the hull.

Normally, the tank is molded without the top or the baffles, and these are glassed to the sides after installation of a handhole, gauge fittings, and required piping in the top panel. Stiffeners may be fabricated on either the outside or the inside. The forms over which these stiffeners (and the baffles) are made may be prelaminated flat sheets of fiberglass cut to the desired shape. Fiberglass tanks are usually cured with heat lamps to drive off any excess styrene in the resin and reduce the possibility of any chemical reaction with the fuel or of any transfer of an objectionable taste to the water.

Installed holding tanks for toilet waste are becoming increasingly commonplace on new boats. Fiberglass tanks can be fabricated to fit the contours of the hull so that the required volume can be obtained with a minimum loss of storage space from the boat.

All tanks should be securely mounted on longitudinal stiffeners or transverse frames. This installation allows adequate support of the hull surface without the concentrated load of the tank, allows free flow of any bilgewater past the tanks, allows better inspection of the tank surfaces, and partially isolates the tanks from impact loads received by the hull. While glass tanks may be overlaid with laminate to the stiffeners, metal tanks may have brackets welded in appropriate locations to facilitate bolting to the framing. If metal tanks are used, most manufacturers prefer aluminum for both fuel and water, but stainless steel may be used for water and mild steel can be used for diesel fuel, if properly painted on the exterior.

When installing metal tanks, it is poor practice to laminate glass over the metal. The glass makes inspection of the condition of the tank almost impossible, and there is no certainty that the glass will remain bonded. When working with tanks or other systems on the boat, every designer, manufacturer, and surveyor should follow the regulations established by the National Fire Protection Association, 60 Batterymarch Street, Boston, Massachusetts 02110, and the recommended practices of the American Boat and Yacht Council Inc., 190 Ketcham Avenue, Amityville, N.Y. 11701.

Rudders

The rudder on any boat is subject to high loading, and not just from the water flow past the rudder surfaces. When a boat is rolling in heavy seas, it can move sideways into the trough of a wave and force the rudder blade into solid water, resulting in large stresses on the rudder stock and heel fitting. This latter fitting is secured to the hull to support the lower end of the rudder and is used on some sailboats and on a few slower commercial powerboats. (See Figure 5.) The rudder stock, or post, is just a steel pipe or a solid round bar about which the blade pivots. It extends inside the hull, where it is attached to the steering system that connects the rudder with the wheel or tiller.

The entire rudder assembly must be well supported inside the hull, usually by a collar that is bolted to the stock and that bears on a solid steel plate and nylon washers, as shown at the top of Figure 5. The inside plate could be a fiberglass laminate fabricated in the shape of a shelf with brackets that are heavily glassed to the hull. Certainly the weight of the rudder should not bear directly on top of the rudder stuffing box, as I have seen on some production powerboats.

FIGURE 5
RUDDER INSTALLATIONS

Rudder with a Heel Fitting and Wheel Steering

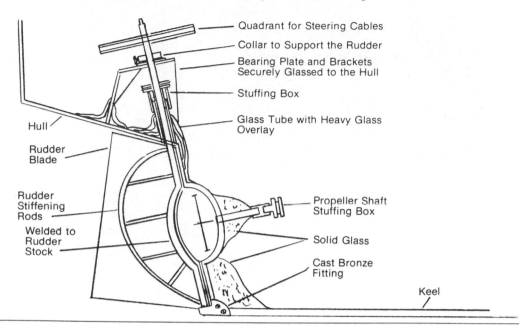

Quadrant for Steering Cables

Collar to Support the Rudder

Bearing Plate and Brackets Securely Glassed to the Hull

Stuffing Box

Glass Tube with Heavy Glass Overlay

Hull

Rudder Blade

Rudder Stiffening Rods

Welded to Rudder Stock

Propeller Shaft Stuffing Box

Solid Glass

Cast Bronze Fitting

Keel

Spade Type Rudder with Tiller Steering

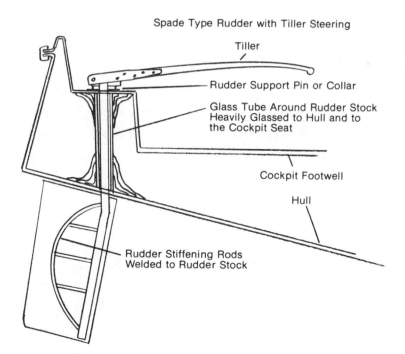

Tiller

Rudder Support Pin or Collar

Glass Tube Around Rudder Stock Heavily Glassed to Hull and to the Cockpit Seat

Cockpit Footwell

Hull

Rudder Stiffening Rods Welded to Rudder Stock

A good installation of a rudder heel fitting on a sailboat. The heel fitting is through bolted to the skeg and the portion projecting aft supports the entire weight of the rudder assembly.

The surveyor's electrical nightmare!

Two sailboat hull molds mounted on rotating cradles so that all areas can be reached by the hull laminators. Note the high gloss of the mold finish.

Some sailboats that have tiller steering and no heel fitting are designed with a fiberglass tube around the rudder post, extending from the hull up to the bottom of the cockpit floor, or seat, which then becomes the load-bearing surface, as shown at the bottom of Figure 5. A pin is secured through a hole in the post, and it bears on a steel ring set on the glass and around the post. This installation is adequate, assuming the pin and rudder post are designed to the proper size. If the rudder is designed without a heel fitting on the bottom— such as spade type rudders used on both sailboats and powerboats— the stock must be designed to withstand both twisting and bending.

The rudder blade on a powerboat is normally of cast or welded metal, but on a sailboat the blade is frequently of molded fiberglass, either solid or with a wood or foamed plastic core. It is most important that a metal rod structure or plate, fabricated from the same material as the rudder stock, be welded to the stock. This forms a stiffening structure for the glass covering and provides a rigid frame to prevent warping. (See Figure 5.) Usually, the stock and stiffening structure are laid into a two-piece mold and the glass is laminated to the proper thickness on both halves before the two are joined. This bonding requires careful workmanship. The two parts must be put together while they are both wet, clamped solidly, and allowed to cure. Because of the relatively thin shapes and the heat given off in the curing process of the fiberglass, the mold and rudder may warp if the entire assembly is not secured rigidly to a workbench or other framework.

If a boat is hard to steer, has more rudder angle on one tack than the other, or has a tendency to veer to one side, be sure to check the straightness of the rudder blade and the stock. Sometimes a sailboat rudder may not have been installed on the centerline of the boat!

Battery Installation

Starting power for a boat engine, or just for lights, is the same as for an automobile, and often boat and auto batteries are interchangeable. But two important differences should be briefly mentioned.

First, the engine and batteries on a boat are normally in a closed, confined space, and second, the boat is regularly subject to rolling and pitching.

All boat batteries should be secured in well-ventilated boxes with removable covers to prevent any metallic object from falling on the terminals. Of course, the acid in the batteries is very dangerous, and the entire battery box assembly must be well fastened to the hull structure. Fiberglass is an excellent material for these boxes.

It is vital to have the boxes and the boat well vented to prevent the accumulation of hydrogen when the batteries are being charged. Remember this when securing the boat at the dock with the battery charger in operation.

The Centerboard

The centerboard or daggerboard of a sailboat may be of various shapes, weights, and sizes, and it presents one of the most important structural problems on the boat. When the board is lowered, the pressure of the water against the side of the blade exerts great force on the portion of the blade that is inside the boat and on the watertight trunk that houses the assembly. In addition, the motion of the boat rolling in a seaway will push the board against one side of the trunk and then the other, possibly loosening any weak joints, depending on the clearance between the board and the trunk. For these reasons, the centerboard trunk must be very strongly laminated into the slot in the hull, and the area between the trunk and the hull should be solid glass mat and resin to a depth of four inches from the bottom.

Some sailors like a very heavy centerboard of bronze or steel, believing that it lowers the center of gravity and increases stability, but this weight is a very small part of the total ballast in the boat and does not have a very great effect. However, the heavy board does produce high stresses at the trunk in a seaway and I prefer the safer installation of a lightweight board fabricated from fiberglass, as the real purpose of the board is to reduce leeway when going to windward.

58

This discussion of fiberglass construction should provide a wealth of detail to guide the owner or surveyor in evaluating the adequacy of a boat—the deck-to-hull joint, attachment of hardware and equipment, major rigging components and mast steps, and overall structural integrity. The following chapter outlines the actual procedures used in the survey.

CHAPTER 5

Survey Procedures

Inspecting a boat is like checking an anchor line or chain; you look at each square inch, trying to find the weakest link. It is impossible to look at the entire hull, or deck, or interior and make any evaluation other than surface appearance. The surveyor should concentrate on one small area of hull, piping, or engine, make a decision, and then move on to an adjacent small area. Often the surveyor cannot inspect the interior surface of the hull because tanks, shower enclosures, the stove, or the icebox blocks the view. These areas should be noted on the survey report, as it is just as important to know what the surveyor could *not* inspect as to know what he did look at.

It is also good practice to inspect by tracing the various systems in the boat. For example, the fuel lines should be traced from the engine fuel pump to the manifold valves, to the tanks and shut-off valves, and to the fill pipe on deck. The vent piping from the tank should also be checked to see that it is in the proper location, as explained later. By actually putting your hands on the piping you can feel whether there are any small leaks, whether the valves are in the right places, and whether the piping is properly secured so that it will not bang around and become damaged.

Similar procedures are outlined in this chapter for inspecting the laminate, the boat exterior, through-hull fittings, interior joinerwork, and mechanical systems: exhaust, engine cooling, electrical, stove, fuel, fresh water, and steering. Special attention should be given to the engine exhaust and steering gear.

Most surveyors have printed forms, or check-off lists, to remind them of each piece of equipment to be observed and each area in which problems have occurred in the past. (Figure 6 is a typical check-

FIGURE 6
SAMPLE CHECK-OFF LIST FOR SURVEYS

Survey for: _____

Boat Name: _____

Date: _____ Location: _____

Boat Type: _____ Monohull or Multihull: _____

L.O.A.: _____ L.W.L.: _____

Beam: _____ Draft: _____

Hull Color: _____ Cabin Color: _____

Year Built: _____ State or Doc. No.: _____

USCG H.I. No.: _____ Home Port: _____

Designer: _____ Builder: _____

Sailboat Data:
  Ballast type
  Centerboard
  Type of rig
  Mast material
  Rigging materials
  Type of reefing
  Number of sails
  Condition of sails
  Sail covers
  Boom material
  Winches

Engineroom Data:
  Engine type
  Number of engines
  Year installed
  Engine model
  Manufacturer
  Horsepower
  Reduction gear
  Shaft size
  Shaft material
  Propeller type
  Struts and bolts
  Shaft stuffing box
  Rudders and supports
  Blower
  Engine beds
  Engine pan
  Exhaust line
  Muffler
  Seacocks
  Bilge pumps
    Manual?

Engineroom Data: (Continued)
  Generator
  Gen. model, KW
  Battery charger
  Shore power
  Appliances
  Batteries, boxes
  Battery ventilation

Hull Exterior:
  Material
  Condition
  Frames
  Flexibility
  Keel
  Transom
  Fastenings
  Through-hulls
  Paint, topsides
  Paint, bottom
  Blisters

Engineroom Data:
  Electrical wiring
  Fuses or circuit breakers
  Bonding system
  Grounded fill on tank
  Fuel tank size and material
  Water tank size and material
  Fire extinguishers
    type and number

Deck:
  Material
  Condition
  Rails

Deck: (*Continued*)
  Windlass
  Anchors
  Nonskid
  Cleats
  Hull joint
  Cabin material and condition
  Portlights
  Dinghy
  Navigation lights
  Steering type and condition
  Quadrant, keyed
  Stuffing box
  Emergency steering
  Lifelines and stanchions
  Bow rail and stern rail

Interior:
  Life jackets
  Bucket
  Flares
  Bilges
  Bulkheads
  Floors
  Ventilation
  Stove
  Stove insulation
  Fuel shut-off
  Refrigeration
  Insulation
  Hot water
  Toilet type
  Vented loop discharge
  Toilet valves
  Shower
  Number of berths
  Lockers
  Drawers
  Hull side covering
  Overhead covering

Interior: (*Continued*)
  Chart desk
  Garbage pail space
  Oilskin locker
  Condition of joinerwork
  Vents to tanks
  Shore polarity indicator
  Hull potential meter
  Centerboard hoist

Equipment List:
  Air conditioning
  Fans
  Television
  Charts
  RDF
  Radiotelephone
  Emergency locator (EPIRB)
  Fathometer
  Speedometer
  Wind direction and speed
  Compass
  Loran
  Radar
  Omega
  Bell, horn
  Barometer
  Searchlight
  Autopilot
  Boarding ladder
  Cockpit cushions
  Fenders
  Fuel gauge
  Cabin heater
  Screens
  Cockpit awning
  Holding tank
  Shower sump pump
  Linens
  Davits on deck

Repairs Necessary at This Time: _____

Estimate of Market Value: _____

Replacement Value: _____

Summary of Surveyor's Opinion of the General Condition of the Boat: _____

_____

_____

off list that may be expanded or condensed as the individual desires.) These forms are convenient but are not complete in themselves and are not a substitute for inspecting each small area of the hull and tracing each installed system.

In addition to the check-off list, the surveyor normally provides the customer with a list of all installed equipment, which can be another preprinted check-off form. This list covers mostly electrical or electronic gear that is present in addition to the normal equipment found on an average boat. It is of primary importance to the buyer, the boat broker, and the insurance company, but it is also a reminder to the surveyor to check for extra equipment on board. It should be emphasized that these lists form only a part of the survey report and that the pages of written comments (see example in Figure 7) are most important in explaining particular discrepancies and recommended repairs.

No one can expect the surveyor to be an expert in internal combustion engines, electronics, and hydraulics, but he should note whether each piece of equipment was in working order at the time of the survey. For example, if the refrigeration system doesn't work, the cause may be a small freon leak or a completely ruined compressor. You can't expect the surveyor to determine the exact problem, but he should call attention to the fact that the refrigeration is not working properly.

Inspecting the Laminate

Fiberglass boats deserve extra attention from the surveyor because of a somewhat unusual situation regarding their construction. In the case of fiberglass, the builder actually manufactures the material used for the hull shell, and his skill and workmanship in putting the laminate together contribute to the integrity of the boat. (The builder of ferrocement boats also manufactures the hull material, but ferrocement makes up a relatively minor portion of the boatbuilding industry.)

By contrast, for metal boats the builder purchases the hull material and must assume that he is receiving a product that has been

FIGURE 7

SAMPLE REPORT OF SURVEY OF A RESIN 30, A 1972 FIBERGLASS
SAILBOAT BUILT BY A.B.C. MARINE, HULL NUMBER 123

Hull:

1. The bottom of the keel is badly gouged from going aground and the aft edge is cracked at the centerline, at the bottom. Repair with epoxy putty and glass overlay both inside and outside.
2. There are numerous deep pits in the propeller shaft and it should be replaced, along with the rubber bearing.
3. The aft edge of the rudder is split. Dry out the rudder and laminate three layers of glass mat over the centerline.
4. There are some minor scratches and gouges on the topsides to starboard. The gel coat is gouged at the stem.

Deck and Rigging:

1. There are some chips in the gel coat around the cockpit seats. Fill with epoxy glue and paint.
2. The cowl for the air vent to port at the transom is at deck level and will allow water to enter the boat. Suggest installation of a water trap type of vent.
3. The running lights are not working at the time of survey. The electronics were not checked.
4. There are cracks in the swaged rigging terminal (lower) on the port forward lower shroud. Replace.
5. The backstay is attached to the masthead assembly with a shackle that is too small. Secure the backstay swaged eye directly to the masthead and use a stainless steel spacer bar at deck level if the stay is too short.
6. The paint has worn off the tops of the wood spreaders and the wood is cracked near the inboard end. Replace with aluminum spreaders.

Mechanical:

1. The engine started easily and ran well but the forward port engine mount is loose. Bolt through the engine bed.
2. The underside of the bridge deck and the exhaust line from the engine to the muffler should be insulated.
3. Could not reach the port seacock on the cockpit scupper drain. Suggest provide access from the quarter berth.
4. There is no strainer in the saltwater line to the engine.
5. The rubber water tank has a split seam.
6. The filler pipe to the fuel tank (gasoline) is not grounded to the boat's bonding system.

Interior:

1. Drill water drain holes in the mast step.
2. Install a shut-off valve in the LP stove gas line between the stove and the companionway.
3. The vinyl hose on the toilet intake line is collapsed. Replace with a rigid hose. Also, there is not a vented loop in the toilet discharge line.
4. Two hanks on the working jib are frozen.
5. The seacock for the toilet sink drain and the bilge pump discharge is frozen and cannot be moved.

Summary: The hull and deck are structurally sound except for the cracks in the keel and the rudder, which require immediate repair. The above listed discrepancies should be repaired without delay.

JOHN DOE INC.
MARINE SURVEYORS

properly manufactured to the correct specifications and is without internal flaws. When he buys aluminum or steel, the builder has to rely on the quality of the mill, and he very seldom inspects the material. Of course, the builder of wood boats must inspect each plank of lumber for natural flaws such as knots and check to see that the plank has been cut from the tree with the correct alignment of grain.

It is often very difficult to inspect the quality of the fiberglass laminate in a finished boat, as the interior is normally painted and the exterior has a color gel coat. Any accidents after manufacture that might have damaged the laminate would show as readily visible cracks or gouges, but what we are discussing at this point is the basic quality of the laminate as fabricated. Three areas are of particular interest to the surveyor in checking the laminate: thickness, the presence of air bubbles (voids), and possible delamination.

Thickness. If the surveyor has a question about the proper thickness of a hull, he should consult the designer to ascertain just what is adequate, as the spacing of the framing must be considered at the same time. It is a mistake to generalize about the thickness of a hull, and the surveyor should not make a definite statement on the question unless he has personally calculated the required laminate and framing.

One guideline can be provided, however, and that is the minimum thickness required for resistance to fracture from impact. Every boat gets pushed against a piling or a dock at some point, and a boat under twenty-five feet in length should have a laminate at least seven-thirty-seconds inch thick at the sheer, increasing in thickness toward the waterline, hull bottom, and keel areas. Larger boats should have a proportionately heavier minimum laminate. This minimum thickness does not guarantee that the boat will not be damaged, of course, as it is possible to fracture any laminate. If the laminate is all glass *mat* (not recommended), the minimum thickness should be greater.

The hull thickness can be measured directly by removing some of the through-hull fittings in different areas on both sides of the boat, and you can readily see whether the builder has done a careful job of laminating by comparing the thickness from one side to the other.

Ultrasonic test equipment is available for thickness measurement, but it is expensive for the average surveyor. The operator also must gain a great deal of experience before his measurements are accurate, and the instrument should be calibrated against a test sample each time it is used. The surveyor is not usually asked to check the hull thickness or evaluate the content of the laminate, and if he is, the removal of a few through-hulls will normally be sufficient. Actually, the surveyor's responsibility is to determine the condition of the laminate and to report any deterioration; he does not necessarily comment on the adequacy of the designer's specifications.

If the designer or manufacturer asks for a sample of the laminate, it is expedient to use a hole saw to make the opening when a new fitting, such as a speedometer or a bilge pump discharge, is to be installed. This is far preferable to cutting a hole that is not needed and that will require an expensive repair. If a burn test is required to determine the glass content, the laminate sample will have to be weighed on a delicate jeweler's scale, as it will normally weigh only a few ounces. Next, the sample is taken outside and the resin is burned away with a gas torch. The remaining glass material is then weighed to determine what percentage is glass and how much was resin. In hand-laminated boat hulls, a 30 percent glass content is considered good, but don't be surprised if the content is as low as 20 percent. Most quality boat builders carefully weigh the glass material and resin before they are laminated into the hull, and these records may be available from the manufacturer, although the surveyor does not normally become involved.

Bubbles. If the interior of the hull shell has not been painted, you can inspect the laminate by shining a normal work lamp on the surface or by using a strong flood lamp outside the hull, assuming that the hull is solid glass laminate without a core. A good laminate shows an even texture and consistency of pattern without spots or areas of a different color. Any voids, or air pockets, that have been trapped in the lamination process will show as white spots that are definitely different from the surrounding area.

A great deal of experience and discretion are called for in this inspection. If the air bubbles appear only over a small area, they are not much cause for concern, but if the surveyor finds a concentrated area of bubbles or one large bubble, some repair is called for. Normally a void can be filled by drilling a small hole into the bubble and inserting epoxy resin with a glue syringe. Larger bubbles near the inside surface are a sign that the laminate was not rolled out sufficiently, and these too should be filled with resin. These inside blisters are not to be confused with outside blisters next to the gel coat, which will be discussed later.

Where the laminate is formed over relatively sharp corners, such as at the sheer or at the transom, there are very likely to be voids, or air pockets, between the gel coat and the laminate. In this case the laminators were not careful to squeeze the first layer of mat tightly against the gel coat. The deck is particularly susceptible to such voids at the cockpit coaming, hatch openings, and molded toerails. Voids can easily be found, as the gel coat is normally cracked around the area. Pushing with a knife on these locations will make the voids very apparent. Fortunately, repairs are also quite easy—just fill with epoxy putty before painting.

Delamination. Delamination is the separation of the plies of the laminate. It may be caused by dirt accumulation, water saturation, excessive stress during the cure, excessive applied loads after the cure, or lack of an initial bond. The initial bond may fail if the laminate was fabricated at different work periods rather than continuously.

Frequently, decks become delaminated when the bond between the laminate and the core fails. Indications of this kind of delamination are excessive flexing and/or a cracking sound as one walks on the deck. It can be repaired by injecting resin through a small hole drilled into the core.

The lack of laminate bond in the hull is harder to detect and is usually found aurally, but sometimes it can be seen by shining a strong lamp through the hull. If you tap the hull with a knife handle, a good laminate will resound with a sharp, hard sound, but a delamination will produce a dull thud. Tapping with a rubber or rawhide mallet or the bottom of your fist will produce the same result. Sometimes you can see the laminate vibrate when hit with a mallet if the delaminated area is large, and this indication, like the flexing of the hull, shows where a repair is required.

The three areas of laminate inspection just discussed—thickness, presence of air bubbles, and possible delamination—are important, but they are often overlooked in the average survey since the glass hull is usually hidden on the interior. Sometimes the exterior may show hairline cracks in the paint or in the more brittle gel coat, which could be an indication of a defective laminate in the interior plies.

Exterior Inspection

An exterior examination should cover the hull, its flexibility, the presence of blisters, the quality of the centerline seam, the rudder, and the condition of the deck.

The surveyor will find that it takes a relatively short period of time to inspect the exterior of the hull and deck on a boat that has not had any damage. Looking for gouges, blisters, pits, and cracks and checking the flexibility and the deck-to-hull joint normally involves less than an hour on a forty-foot boat. A much longer time will be spent looking at the interior, the installed systems, and the equipment. This does not mean, however, that the hull should be glanced over quickly, as there are often flaws in an otherwise glossy and good-looking surface.

The Hull. When you first approach the boat, stand some distance away and check the overall smoothness of the surface. Look for a high gloss in the finish, as dullness is a sign of careless molding or lack of maintenance. The sunlight will eventually deteriorate the gel coat, just as it affects ordinary paint, and the fiberglass should be waxed twice a year to build up a protective coating.

The sheerline should be a smooth curve from bow to stern; any bumps are a sign that the deck and hull do not fit together correctly. Vertical lines or creases in the exterior finish occur where bulkheads or joinerwork has been fitted too tightly to the hull before bonding with strips of glass material. Such deformities can be avoided by laminating three layers of mat to the hull to form a pad about six inches wide at the edge of the bulkhead.

Any areas of the hull that are concave, or "dished in," should be carefully checked. This condition can develop if the framing inside the shell is too widely spaced or if the shell laminate is too thin so that the continuous fairness of the hull is obviously not maintained. Sometimes these concave spots appear in the topsides just below the shroud chainplates on a sailboat. They result when the chainplate attachment to the hull extends over too small an area to distribute the load properly. To distribute the load, a large glass knee at least two feet in height can be overlaid to both the underside of the deck and the hull, as explained earlier.

Any scratches, nicks, or gouges in the exterior gel coat should be noted. These can be filled with epoxy glue, or epoxy putty, to insure watertightness. It is especially important to look at the bottom of the keel to see whether past groundings have produced gouges that extend into the basic laminate. Any penetration deeper than the gel coat will allow water to enter and will eventually cause delamination. These areas must be chiseled out to a dry laminate, then repaired with epoxy putty. Usually the keel blocks will have to be moved so that the entire keel area can be checked carefully.

Hairline cracks often appear in the gel coat on both hull and deck surfaces, especially at corners of the cabin top. These are usually a sign of applied stress, some of which may have occurred when the part was removed from the mold. If these fine cracks appear to be only as deep as the gel coating, there is usually no structural problem, just a cosmetic one. But if these cracks are wide and have penetrated the laminate, a repair is definitely necessary. Often these hairline cracks show on areas of the hull where the surface is relatively flat and without much curvature, such as forward just at the waterline, on both powerboats and sailboats. In these forward areas, the hull shell has probably been flexing repeatedly, or "oil canning," as the boat pounds into the waves. Eventually the laminate will be cracked all the way through the hull.

All through-hull fittings should be examined to see whether the thickness of the metal has been reduced by corrosion, or whether the surface has been pitted. Propellers, rudders, struts, and shafts should be inspected for the same conditions. Some alloys of stainless steel become badly pitted in salt water, and the surveyor would do well to look for this problem.

It is difficult for the surveyor to decide what condition is cause for rejection and what can be tolerated for a longer period of time. This question applies not only to corrosion, but to paint, hairline cracks, blisters, chafing, and excessive flexing of the hull shell. For example, can a one-sixteenth-inch pit in a propeller shaft be overlooked but not a one-eighth-inch pit? What if there is just one pit and not several? If the hull gel coat has a hairline crack, will it progress into the laminate? These are hard questions and can probably best be answered by saying that any crack, pit, or discontinuity can form a stress riser that may precipitate a failure. It is the surveyor's job to point out these defects and to assume that the boat will have hard and continuous service, rather than just sitting at the dock. Therefore, all defective areas should be repaired or the parts replaced, as they will surely reach the point of failure over a period of time.

Flexibility. We have discussed the necessity for framing behind the hull shell and noted that excessive flexing will result in cracks through the laminate. Testing for this flexibility, or lack of stiffness, requires considerable judgment and can best be accomplished by hitting the hull surface with a rubber or rawhide mallet or the side of your fist. In doing this you will feel and see excessive movement where the framing is too widely spaced. Many boats with inner liners that are not securely glassed to the hull will exhibit this flexing, showing that additional stiffening is necessary.

Normally the boat is sitting in a cradle with side supports, and a flat spot in the hull will be apparent at these supports if framing is insufficient. Sometimes these side supports are not tight against the hull, however, and it is good practice to make sure they are secured, not only for safety reasons but to see whether a flat spot will develop. If the side supports have screw jacks, you can extend them tightly against the hull while watching for any deflection. This must be done carefully, however, so that the center of gravity of the boat is not

71

moved. If a boat is well stiffened, the keel will lift off the blocks slightly before the hull has flexed at the side supports.

If the laminate has been damaged by accident, there will usually be some hairline cracks on the surface—sometimes circular around the point of impact, and sometimes in a straight line, parallel to the stiffener about which the hull has been flexing. These can be spotted easily from the outside, and a further, detailed inspection both inside and out is required to determine whether structural damage has occurred.

Blisters. Antifouling paint is always necessary on the bottom of a fiberglass boat if it is kept in the water, and the best advice on paint application is to follow the manufacturer's instructions carefully, no matter what brand of paint you purchase. It is especially important to use a primer, or undercoat, that is formulated specifically for the brand of paint that will be applied later.

Blisters may appear below the waterline on a glass hull between the gel coat and the first layer of mat in the laminate. These blisters may be as small as a dime or as large as three inches in diameter, and they may occur singly or in clusters over all or a small portion of the hull.

It is not exactly clear how these blisters develop, but it is believed that a chemical interaction produces a gas bubble under the gel coat, either at the time of molding or much later after the antifouling paint is applied and the boat is in the water. It is also possible that water enters minute pinholes in the polyester gel coat that were formed during the curing process of the hull.

Most objective observers in the boating industry agree that these blisters are not harmful, nor do they reduce boat speed if they are intact, because they do not grow in size, but some owners insist that they be ground off the hull for purely cosmetic reasons. If the blisters have broken open and the laminate is exposed, the area will have to be sanded, dried, and filled with epoxy putty before painting.

Centerline Seams. The centerline of the hull should be smooth and even with no irregular humps of gel coat or voids where the gel coat is missing entirely. At times, a hull that has been molded in two pieces and not joined correctly will exhibit a hairline crack on centerline where the surface has not been faired properly. This crack should be ground open and filled with epoxy putty, unless the crack extends into the laminate, in which case further repairs would be required.

Not all hulls molded in two pieces are necessarily suspect, however, as they can be structurally excellent if proper care is taken when molding. The builder should mold only the gel coat and a lightweight mat within twenty-four inches of centerline in each half of the mold, and when the halves are joined the remainder of the laminate can be laid down in one piece, extending over a wide area. Because this technique requires great care and later finishing of the centerline seam, most builders prefer to mold the hull in one piece. The reason for using a two-part hull mold is so that the laminating crew can reach across the mold to roll out the glass fabric without stepping into the mold or lying on a scaffold.

The Rudder. Since the rudder is normally molded in two halves, it, like the hull, should be carefully inspected on centerline. Sometimes the rudder blade is hollow rather than filled with a core material, and it could be full of water if there is a centerline crack. While this condition is not of immediate concern, the rudder should be drained, dried, filled with foam or solid glass, and repaired before delamination can begin.

Fiberglass rudders are principally found on sailboats, as the cast bronze rudders usually found on powerboats are too heavy and expensive. The rudder on a sailboat is normally much larger than that on a powerboat, as the sailboat moves at much lower speeds and does not have as great a water flow past the blade. Therefore, a larger area is needed to provide adequate steering control under all conditions.

The Deck. Walking on the deck and cabin top with a heavy tread will usually show any inherent flexibility and will reveal where additional deck stiffening is required. Flexible areas must be inspected from the inside to determine whether access to the underside of the

There are at least ten items for a surveyor to inspect in this sailboat cockpit.

1. Do the cockpit seat hatches have drain grooves to keep water from flowing into the bilges?

2. Is the laminate of the cockpit sole and seats rigid enough so that there is no flexing when a person jumps on it?

3. Is the cockpit sole braced to the hull with partial bulkheads?

4. Is the steering pedestal and guard rail through bolted with backing plates?

5. Are the cleats and winches through bolted with backing plates?

6. Are the ventilator openings properly ducted to the low point of the bilge?

7. Is the stern rail through bolted and are the individual sections properly welded or bolted?

8. The backstay turnbuckle should be pinned to prevent rotation and there should be a toggle just below the turnbuckle.

9. The mainsheet traveller should be through bolted.

10. Are there any voids in the glass laminate or cracks in the gel coat?

deck can be attained so that deck beams or vertical supporting posts to the hull can be installed. Sometimes a molded glass headliner covers the deck, or a post interferes with the passageway. In this case, it may be necessary to fabricate a curved arch secured to the hull side and fit tightly to the overhead.

Often the cockpit seats and the footwell area are not supported from beneath, and rough pounding and rolling in a seaway induce flexing and twisting of the cockpit area that can be felt while sitting at the helm. In this situation, partial bulkheads must be glassed to the hull and the underside of the cockpit and to the bottom of the side decks wherever possible. Common fir two-by-four planks can also be glassed to the hull and footwell to support the entire structure.

Interior Inspection

The interior inspection should include the forepeak areas; the inside of the deck-to-hull joint, keel cavity, propeller shaft, and rudder post; through-hull fittings; and joinerwork.

Forward Areas. When he begins his interior inspection, the surveyor checks the forepeak area for any sign of cracking of the interior paint or laminate that may have resulted from excessive flexing. The hull sides are normally almost flat in this area with little stiffness as a result of curvature of shape. Longitudinal stiffeners from the stem to the forepeak bulkhead may be required.

The anchor line may be inspected and removed to see whether any water has collected under the coils. All deck fittings should be checked from the underside to see whether any leaks have left water or rust streaks on the hull. Most important, it is necessary to see that the headstay chainplate has been properly through-bolted with a backing plate and threads that have been staked so the nut will not back off. As mentioned earlier, the tack plate on deck should have a backing plate strap extending down to the headstay chainplate bolts so that the loading of the jib is transferred to the hull rather than tending to pull the deck away from the hull. If the electrical wiring for the running lights is located here, look for signs of water leaks that would lead to an electrical short circuit.

Deck-to-Hull Joint.   Next, the surveyor checks the attachment of the deck to the hull all around the sheer, from the inside. Whatever the configuration of the joint, the two parts should be bolted together before glassing and the seam of the joint should be filled with glass mat or a permanent bedding compound. When subject to rough-water operation, this hull and deck seam is twisted so much that fastenings may eventually be loosened. If the joint is poor, water leaks may be evident around the bolts and rub rail fastenings. On better boats, this joint is covered with three layers of glass mat and two layers of woven roving, which effectively bond the deck and hull permanently into a one-piece structure.

This sheer area cannot be given too careful attention, as it is usually the location where the rub rail is attached and where the boat makes contact if it bangs against dock pilings. At the same time the sheer area is inspected on a sailboat, the remaining rigging chainplates can be checked to see that there has not been any movement of the assembly or overstressing of the deck in particular. Many times, a water leak will be the evidence of chainplate movement.

Below the Waterline.   The surveyor should keep in mind those areas of a boat that get the most wear, or abuse—the areas where he always finds problems on any type of hull. The bottom of the keel always gets gouged, and hairline cracks may not be readily visible from outside the hull. A careful inside inspection of the keel area aft of the ballast will reveal any small water leaks. This keel cavity normally contains some bilgewater, which must be drained for closer inspection if it is at all possible to get near this area.

The stuffing boxes located at the propeller shaft and the rudder post normally do a good job of keeping the water out with the packing gland, but their attachment to the glass hull sometimes presents a difficult construction problem. Whether there is a glass tube or a bolted casting at these stuffing boxes, the hull should be inspected for cracks and water leaks. If the glass tube is more than eighteen inches in length, it should be supported by glass brackets to the hull in addition to being heavily glassed at the hull opening.

Through-Hull Fittings. All through-hull fittings are certainly checked by any surveyor to see that the attached valves are working properly, but it is just as important to see that the fitting itself is securely attached to the hull. Normally, a through-hull fitting is a threaded bronze sleeve with a flange on the outside; it is inserted through a hole in the hull and secured with a large nut on the inside. It usually has a valve, or seacock, threaded to it, and carries water in or out of the boat. (Examples are sink drains, toilet intake and discharge, engine cooling water intake, and cockpit scupper drains.) Obviously, these fittings are of prime importance, as the crew must have a positive method of closing off these holes in the hull in case of a leak or failure of the hose line inside the boat.

There have been many cases of a careless crew or yard worker stepping on a valve and overstressing the material in the fitting or bending the relatively thin glass hull to the point of fracture. To prevent this, the hole in the hull must be reinforced with a glass or wood block on the inside before the fitting is inserted. This is especially true with flush-mounted through-hull fittings as found on sailboats, where the glass hull is beveled around the hole. In fact, the flush fitting is not recommended unless the hull thickness is doubled over an area twelve inches square by laminating extra glass around the inside of the hole. In all installations, a seacock rather than a standard valve is recommended, as a proper seacock has provisions for lubricating the internal parts without dismantling and it has a solid base for attachment to the reinforced area of the hull rather than being supported only by the threaded through-hull fitting.

Interior Joinerwork. All the bulkheads, partial bulkheads, berth bottoms, and locker sides are secured to the hull by glass overlay, or bonding, and all this glass work should be checked to see that the bond is still good. If these areas are loose, they should be glassed again, and looseness may be a sign that the hull has been stressed in that locality and the laminate should be checked for hairline cracks.

The quality of wood craftsmanship can be discussed at great length, but it can probably best be summarized in terms of the original cost of the boat. The least expensive hulls have painted woodwork with the edge grain of the plywood bulkheads covered with a glued vinyl trim, while the better boats have wood veneers on the bulkheads and solid, varnished wood trim. The buyer does get exactly what he pays for, and the surveyor should realize this fact.

All the wood parts should be glassed to the hull or screwed to each other; staples and nails are signs of carelessness. If the joiner-work is subassembled away from the boat and then fastened to the wood or glass cabin flooring, it should be bolted and not screwed, because screws can loosen from vibration and twisting.

The surveyor should check any holes in the wood structure that support electrical wiring or piping, as continued vibration may cause the wood to wear through the plastic materials, unless there is a plastic bushing at the hole. When the wood joinerwork extends below the cabin sole, it should be glassed to the hull completely to form a watertight seal around the wood, as it can develop rot when water-soaked.

If the boat has an icebox, it should be surrounded on all six sides with at least four inches of insulation. This is difficult for the surveyor to check, but sometimes he can see the area between the hull and the box. Also, any icebox drain should have a valve so that the cold water is trapped in the box to help the ice last. Many experienced skippers prefer to pump the water from the icebox directly overboard with a small hand pump rather than have an installed drain line, as the water may contain bits of food and should not be left in the bilges.

Mechanical Systems Inspection

In describing the survey of equipment and engines in a boat, one could write hundreds of pages and duplicate the owner's manual for each piece of equipment installed, but we will not go into much detail here except to say that each component should be checked for proper operation and referred to a factory-authorized repairman if found to be inoperative. The surveyor can never be sure of the agreements between the owner and the dealer, and he should not tamper with any equipment lest he affect some warranty arrangement.

However, the surveyor should examine each piece of hardware, wiring, and piping aboard with a critical eye in addition to taking a broad overview of the entire system. For example, each engine has a lubrication system, a gearbox, exhaust lines, a fuel system, controls, electrical components, and a cooling water system. The surveyor should inspect each piece of the assembly in addition to running the engine for a few minutes to observe the overall operation. If he has any question about the condition of the engine, generator, air compressor, or refrigeration, he should recommend a complete inspection by a competent mechanic.

Exhaust System. The exhaust line from the engineroom to the transom is often hidden behind lockers or berths and is difficult to inspect thoroughly. However, it is one of the most important items on the boat, as serious problems can result if the exhaust leaks into a living area, whether the system is a dry exhaust or whether the engine cooling water is drained into the system. The important point in both installations is to look for loose connections between the sections of pipe or hose, and corrosion of the piping at elbows or bends. When an iron pipe is badly rusted, it is always good practice to recommend replacement of the section, and it is always good form to poke the corroded area with the tip of a knife to see if a hole can be made. If the wall is so thin that a hole does appear, the pipe should have been replaced before that time. Look for discolored streaks indicating a water leak or dripping at each joint throughout the exhaust line. A dry exhaust, or a wet exhaust at the engine, will require asbestos insulation to prevent burns to the crew and to prevent the wood joinerwork and decks from becoming overheated or burned during continuous operation.

In a wet exhaust, the high sulphur content of the fuel residue apparently corrodes most metals in the high-temperature exhaust collector section close to the engine before the water is injected into the line. Cast iron is one of the better metals to use in this application, but almost any system has to be replaced every few years. Non-metallic materials can usually be used only in the low-temperature sections after the water is combined with the exhaust.

Even though the exhaust port at the transom is above the water-line, wave action at the stern can result in water entering the opening, especially in a following sea. For this reason, all sections of the system must slope down from the high point at the engine. Pipe hangers should support the exhaust line every four feet to prevent vibration from loosening the joints, and these supports should be padded so that they do not wear through.

Engine Cooling. Many overheating problems with engines and generators are caused by a restriction in the water intake line, and this section of piping between the hull opening and the equipment should be examined very carefully. Often, some debris or a plastic bag will become lodged in the through-hull fitting and will have to be removed from outside the hull. I have seen a serious overheating problem occur as a result of weeds becoming wedged together at an elbow fitting between the water intake seacock and the water strainer. In a case like this, the strainer will appear perfectly clear and the problem will not become apparent until the piping is dismantled. For this reason, it is poor practice to use elbows to make bends in seawater piping. Any bends should be accomplished by using bent pipe or gently curving hose. For some reason, installation mechanics want to use elbows on each side of the seawater strainer, and this practice should be eliminated.

Some builders do not install a seacock at the salt water intake through-hull fitting, reasoning that someone may start the engine with the valve closed. This, also, is dangerous. If a leak occurs in the piping, the crew will have to try to install a wood plug in the piping that is still intact. A better solution is to install a seacock but lock-wire the handle in the open position.

Electrical Systems. The electrical demand varies widely from boat to boat, and all the surveyor can do is check for proper installation of wiring and circuit breakers rather than determine whether the system has been adequately designed for the electrical requirements of the installed equipment. Frayed insulation, lack of support for the wiring, and wiring soaked with bilgewater should all be noted. Many kinds of plastic clips for electrical wiring are available on the market in sizes for individual wires or large bundles. These clips should be used to hold the wiring in position, attached with a screw fastener into the wood on one side of the wire. The use of staples around the wire should be avoided.

Many times, the careless addition of equipment after the boat has been in service will result in the addition of circuits to an existing circuit breaker, increasing the amperage to a level well above the protection provided. Even worse, new equipment may be wired to the power supply without benefit of a circuit breaker. This error can be found by checking the nameplates on the electrical panel to make sure there is a circuit breaker (or fuse) for each appliance. Often overlooked is the recommended practice of installing circuit breakers in the A.C. shore power supply lines physically close to the main supply location in order to protect all wiring within the boat.

It is important for the direct current (D.C.) appliances to be grounded with a common wire that itself is connected to the negative side of the power supply. This battery D.C. supply is normally 12 volts but is determined by the starting motor voltage required for the main engine. Sailboats normally have the most problems with battery power, as sailors have a tendency to draw down batteries without recharging them by running the engine. For this reason, it is important to have at least two batteries with the circuits divided so that one battery serves only the main engine. Modern boat owners also tend to equip their boats with a speedometer, fathometer, searchlight, electric horn, wind direction and speed indicators, and stereo tape system, and all of these, added to the cabin and navigation lights and bilge blower, tend to deplete the charge on a battery in just a few hours. Electrical shorts commonly develop in the equipment just mentioned due to water leaks or improper installation. About all the surveyor can be expected to do is list the device as operating or out of order.

It is good practice for the surveyor to read the American Boat and Yacht Council standards and the National Fire Protection Association regulations frequently and to refer to these publications when writing the report of survey.

Stoves. Many types of stoves using various fuels are available for marine use, but a few rules apply to all of them. Stove installations should be well ventilated, and the joinerwork or deck over the stove should be covered with asbestos to prevent overheating. When purchasing a stove, it is well to check the oven sides to make sure they are well insulated and to ascertain that replacement parts are available for the burners.

When liquefied petroleum (LP) gas stoves are used, the owner should post a readily visible sign explaining the proper operation and precautions, as the gas is heavier than air and is explosive. Every attempt must be made to keep the gas from collecting in the bilges by frequent inspection for leaks, and a master shut-off valve must be located in the gas supply line between the stove and the companionway exit ladder in case of a burner malfunction. Even though each LP-gas bottle has an installed valve, which must be closed when the boat is vacant, particular care must be taken in the installation of these bottles. They are required to be in gastight compartments, separate from the rest of the boat, with an overboard vent line at the bottom of each compartment. Of course, a match should *never* be used to check for leakage in the fittings and piping. The approved method is to spread a soap solution over the piping; a bubble will form over any area where gas is leaking out.

Fuel Systems. Most problems in the fuel system—whether a gasoline or a diesel system for a main engine or a generator—occur because of loose fittings at the piping sections, loose tank mountings, or lack of support for the piping. All the piping between the tank and the engine should be inspected, particularly at fuel filters and valves, to see that piping brackets are located close enough to prevent vibration damage. The fill pipe to the deck should be grounded to the tank and to the boat's electrical bonding (grounding) system in order to eliminate any spark of static electricity when the fuel hose from a pump on the dock touches the boat's fill pipe.

All piping connections must be made on the top of the tank in order to reduce the possibility of draining the tank accidentally, and any transfer of fuel from one tank to another should be accomplished by a pump rather than by gravity. Of course, any tank requires a vent pipe to an outside point above the deck, and any diesel tank needs a return line for fuel flow from the engine to the tank.

Fresh Water Systems. Any boat is subject to a great deal of pounding and vibration, and these loads can cause loose tanks and piping connections. As with fuel systems, the surveyor should look at the tank beds and mountings and check every pipe joint, valve, and supporting hanger. If the boat has a pressure supply pump rather than a hand pump at each sink, the surveyor should check for operation and leaks and see that any flexible hose is designed for the system pressure. Very often, a nonreinforced plastic hose will collapse when the pump is in operation. If a hot water tank is installed, it usually receives the hot water from the main engine's cooling system and heats fresh water in a shell and tube heat exchanger. An electric A.C. heating coil is installed for use when the main engine is not in operation. All the piping to this heater, especially the engine water lines, must be carefully checked for leakage or corrosion.

Plastic piping is now widely used in fresh water systems, and it has given good service in most applications. Still, the surveyor must look for adequate support for the piping, leaks at the joints, and use of the correct type of plastic for hot water lines. If this plastic piping is accidentally stepped on, the joints, which are glued with solvent, may open, and leaks may appear. Leaks of this kind are sometimes difficult to detect unless you are actually looking at the faulty section of pipe while water is running.

I once found a plastic fitting on a plastic water tank that had a large deposit of epoxy glue around the exterior circumference, apparently from a previous repair. Since the tank was empty and the water available at the boatyard was not drinkable, I did not want to fill the tank and test the system for leaks. Unfortunately, I forgot to mention this on the survey report. As might be expected, the new owner was slightly upset some weeks later to find out that the tank fitting leaked; the tank had not been used in over a year; and the entire tank had to be replaced. Such are the surprises in the life of a surveyor. Nothing can be taken for granted. Every fitting is suspect, and if something can possibly malfunction, it probably will.

Steering Systems. Every boat should have an alternate method of steering in case the primary installed system fails. Many times, this backup consists of a tiller and extension made from steel pipe that fits through a deck plate and attaches to the top of the rudder post. Even a small sailboat that has a wood tiller should carry a spare wood substitute and an extra tiller head fitting. The primary steering system connecting the steering wheel with the rudder post may use a direct pipe linkage, hydraulics, a heavy "push-pull" type of cable within a sleeve, or conventional wire rope and sheaves. If an auto-pilot is installed, the surveyor should simply determine whether the gear in fact turns the rudder, and if not, recommend that a factory repairman be consulted. The steering gear should be observed while someone is turning the wheel and the autopilot.

While looking at the rudder tiller arm, or quadrant, the alignment of the system components should be checked, as any binding or friction between parts will eventually result in failure. This is particularly important in a system using wire rope over sheaves, and any evidence of bronze shavings or powder usually means that the sheave is not correctly positioned. Of course, the quadrant must be keyed to the rudder post and rudder stops should be installed to prevent the rudder from hitting the hull or to prevent damage to the steering gear.

If the boat is making long ocean passages, an alternate steering method—such as a long steering oar that can be mounted on the stern—should be available. Since storage space is limited, the oar can be fabricated in three sections with a length of pipe in the middle. Often the steering gear fails but the rudder and post are still intact, and the crew can steer by rigging lines from each side of the boat to the rudder blade, attaching them to an eye fitting or through a hole.

The wide variety of systems and equipment installed on modern boats presents a challenge to the surveyor and he often encounters system problems and equipment defects that he has not seen previously. If the surveyor makes a note of these unusual problems on his survey check list, he will be able to conduct a more efficient survey and reduce the number of surprises that make a surveyor's life both interesting and frustrating.

CHAPTER 6

Questions Most Often Asked the Surveyor

An owner or prospective buyer often asks the surveyor a multitude of questions during the course of a survey, and some are not entirely related to the job at hand. This chapter describes some of the most interesting questions that I have heard.

1. *I have a chance to buy a boat that sank. It is sitting on the bottom in six feet of water. It has twin diesel engines and is loaded with electronics. Is it a good buy?*

Answer: Usually it is a "good-bye"! A sunken boat can normally be raised by local scuba divers, but this must be accomplished within a few hours of the accident to prevent permanent damage to the engines and electrical equipment.

Even if the boat is raised immediately, the engines must be taken apart to inspect for internal corrosion and to remove water contamination of the lubricating oil passages. Electrical outlets become filled with water and rusting starts wherever water is allowed to become trapped. Electrical insulation around wiring may be destroyed when water enters the end of the wire and travels through the insulation by capillary action. Any equipment that becomes watersoaked, especially if it is electronic, must be completely dismantled, dried, and cleaned.

Watersoaked wood joinerwork will become stained and may have to be refinished if not replaced. This is especially true of plywood, as water can enter the edge grain and travel between the plies. Of course,

87

upholstery, carpeting, curtains, clothes, and food will probably be ruined. If a surveyor is hired to inspect a boat that has been sunk, the job is much more difficult and requires careful attention to detail. For example, the expensive batteries will normally be shorted and will require replacement.

Usually the fiberglass hull and deck will have no damage except at the hole (if any) that caused the sinking. Assuming the prospective buyer of a sunken hull has permission from the owner and his insurance company to raise the hull, he must then carefully weigh his costs of buying the hull together with the repairs required and a great deal of hard work. At the worst, he may have to replace everything in the boat except hull, deck, hardware, and ballast.

2. *What do I do if my boat is in a collision and the hull is cracked below the waterline?*

Answer: The first problem, of course, is to stop the flow of water and to keep the boat afloat. This can best be accomplished by putting a "collision mat" over the bow of the boat and sliding it aft until it is over the crack. The mat is nothing more than a piece of heavy canvas, about four feet square, with grommets and four lines tied to the corners. One side of the canvas can be covered with foam rubber or tufts of manila rope "baggywrinkle" that is placed against the hull in an attempt to slow the water flow. The water pressure against the mat does not completely stop the leak, and some additional work inside the hull is necessary. If the crack is wide enough, it can be stuffed with rags, a mattress, or rubber. Normally, a crack in a glass hull is thin and can be hard to find. It is best sealed with underwater epoxy putty. After the water flow is stopped, a temporary repair can be made to the inside by laminating glass to a clean, roughened, dry surface until the boat can be hauled out for a more permanent repair.

When a hull is cracked in an accident, the damage usually occurs well forward where the boat has hit a rock or half-submerged log. However, in a sailboat a crack may develop just under the mast if the mast foundation is not wide enough to distribute the load adequately. In the latter case, a collision mat can usually be rigged under

Inspection of a cast iron bolted keel. The lifting straps are shown under the keel center of gravity, and the seam at the top of the keel shows some separation.

Note the grounding wire secured to the rudder stuffing box to guard against electrolysis and for lightning protection.

the hull, but it is difficult to reach the inside of the crack, as the mast step is in the way. About all you can do is take down the sails and slacken the rigging turnbuckles two turns. This takes the compression load off the mast and thus will keep the crack from opening farther. It is not good to slacken the rigging too much, as the mast then may pound vertically as the boat slams into a rough seaway. If the entire mast support has collapsed, the rigging may well be too slack and must be tightened to keep the mast on the foundation, after underwater epoxy has been squeezed into the crack underneath.

3. *Can full flotation be provided to make a boat unsinkable?*

Answer: Yes. You can use foamed plastic, cork, air tanks, or balsa wood for flotation. It must be secured in the hull below the flooded waterline, or final line of flotation. Individual air tanks must be kept small, as one might be punctured during an accident, or an inspection plate may not be completely watertight. Also, you could use a system of inflatable air bags, similar to life rafts, that could be inflated inside the hull if an accident occurs. These bags should not completely fill the hull interior; a passageway should be left on centerline so the crew can have access to the bilge and make an attempt to find and stop the leak.

Any flotation material will take up space otherwise used for storage. Thus, providing full flotation becomes a greater problem on a small boat than on a larger one. Every piece of material in the hull contributes something toward flotation, as any material weighs less in water than in air. The relative underwater weight of a material is found by subtracting the density of water from the density of the particular material. Of course, if the material has a density less than that of water, it will float. So it is easy to see that a wood hull requires less flotation material than a steel hull, and that an unballasted power boat requires less flotation than a sailboat with a heavy lead keel. The amount of required flotation material differs widely, and each hull must be considered carefully.

It is not difficult for the boat designer to calculate the amount of flotation material required, as he has already estimated the weight of each item in the boat prior to drawing the lines of the hull. The purpose of this weight estimate is to design the hull to a correct total displacement and to make sure the boat is floating level at its designed waterline. Also, the vertical position of the center of gravity, which is necessary for stability calculations, is determined from this weight estimate. The weight of each item in the boat is divided by the density of that particular material and the resulting volumes, in cubic feet, are totaled and subtracted from the displacement of the hull, also in cubic feet. The resulting volume, which should be calculated for each hull, is the amount of flotation required. It is not good practice to estimate or generalize about the amount of flotation needed, but for preliminary purposes, a ballasted sailboat requires about 55 to 65 percent of the total displacement for flotation, and an unballasted power boat will require about 10 percent less.

It would certainly seem good insurance to make your boat unsinkable, especially if you are going on long ocean passages. It is undoubtedly worth the extra cost of a longer hull and the flotation material. In fact, it is my personal opinion that most boats should be designed with the additional volume to accommodate full flotation. It is indeed unfortunate that the recent trend in boat interiors is to fill up every cubic foot with berths and electrical appliances instead of concentrating on necessary aspects of boat operation and safety. Finally, it may be well to note that in calculating flotation, the weight of the flotation material itself should be added to the boat weight so that an accurate volume is obtained. Also, the weight of filled tanks must be included in total displacement, as they cannot be considered as air tanks that provide total buoyancy.

4. *Do you think the existing propeller is right for this boat?*

Answer: The selection of a propeller size is affected by the engine horsepower, rpm's, reduction gear, volume of hull, and space available to fit the propeller. These considerations fall into the designer's province, and the surveyor would normally avoid the problem unless he is unusually experienced. He would probably refer the owner to a local propeller shop, the boat manufacturer, or a naval architect.

91

More often, an owner will ask about the use of a three-bladed propeller on a sailboat or a four-bladed propeller on a powerboat. The sailboat presents a particular problem, as the sailor wants minimal drag, thus no propeller, when under sail, but he must have a propeller when maneuvering around the dock. The least drag occurs with a two-bladed propeller, and even less is apparent if the propeller is allowed to rotate when sailing. Rotation is not allowed, however, if the sailboat is racing. If you want to allow the propeller to turn, you must make sure that the transmission on the engine will allow free shaft rotation when the engine is not running. Sometimes there is not sufficient oil lubrication of the gears and damage will result.

When a two-bladed propeller is locked for sailing, it should be aligned vertically behind the keel or strut for minimum drag. If a sailboat is going to be powering most of the time, such as on rivers, the three-bladed propeller is more efficient, as it has greater blade area to transmit the torque of the engine to thrust in the water. In fact, many owners change propellers during a cruise or when changing from long periods of sailing to powering. The two-bladed propeller is normally two inches greater in diameter than the three-bladed, as the propeller load should allow the engine to rotate at the maximum rated rpm, but no faster.

Some sailboats use a two-bladed folding propeller for minimum drag while racing, but these have too little blade area to be efficient under power, particularly in a heavy boat, and many skippers change the propeller when a race has finished. Probably the ideal compromise, especially for a larger boat, is the feathering propeller, which is more common in Europe and is more costly. By using internal linkages inside a hollow propeller shaft, the pitch of the blades can be varied with the desired speed and with the load carried (the weight of the boat). The skipper of a sailboat would align the blades fore-and-aft for sailing and yet have the correct pitch available when under power; similarly, the captain of a fishing boat would vary the pitch depending on whether the boat was empty and running free or fully loaded and going slowly.

Recreational powerboat propellers are normally of the three-bladed type in smaller, faster boats under forty feet in length, while heavy boats and larger boats usually employ the four-bladed propeller.

5. *What can I do to prevent electrolysis?*

Answer: Electrolysis, or electro-galvanic corrosion, affects only metals, so a fiberglass hull will not be corroded. At times, a bronze propeller or a stainless steel propeller shaft will show pitting that may be caused by stray electrical currents emanating from the shore power. Ask to have the grounded conductor on the shore power checked to make sure that it is in fact grounded close to your dock. Also, hang a block of zinc in the water with a no. 8 wire connecting it to the boat's bonding system. In addition, small zinc pads can be bolted to the rudder, close to the propeller. The stainless shaft or strut may become pitted, but from other forms of corrosion than electrolysis, and the correct alloy should be chosen for marine shafting. Steel manufacturers distribute stainless shafts specifically for marine use.

Problems with electrolysis are more prevalent in steel or aluminum boats, and a hull potential meter should be installed for monitoring any stray currents. In addition, the shore power connection should be made through an isolation transformer. No bronze, copper, or lead fittings should be used, and the antifouling paint for metal hulls must not contain any copper or mercury compounds. Be sure to read the paint can labels!

6. *Where should the rudder be located?*

Answer: The rudder should be directly aft of the propeller so that the water flow is directed onto the rudder blade for maximum turning effort. On a powerboat, the blade may be offset one or two inches from the shaft centerline to allow the shaft to be removed without dropping the rudder. On a sailboat, however, the rudder must be exactly on the centerline of the boat. In section, the rudder is often shaped like an airfoil, but on very high-speed powerboats the rudder section usually is wedge-shaped, with the narrow edge forward.

The rudder location on a powerboat is not subject to much discussion; it can be under the hull or mounted aft on a transom bracket. Sailboat rudders, however, have been placed in a wide variety of locations, all of which have been reasonably successful. For many years, the keel on a sailboat was extended to the aft end of the waterline and the rudder was hung on the trailing edge of the keel. This arrangement worked very well, but the modern trend is toward shorter keels with less wetted surface for lower resistance, and if the rudder were at the after end of the keel, it would be too far forward for efficiency. The reason for the inefficiency is that the boat turns around a point close to the middle of the hull, and the short lever arm between the rudder blade and the turning point produces an insufficient turning moment. Obviously, the rudder must be farther aft to be efficient. With the longer turning arm, the area of the rudder can be reduced and still produce a sufficient turning force.

Many modern boats, therefore, have a small rudder configuration close to the waterline. Unfortunately, with this arrangement, most of the rudder is out of water when the boat is heeled over, and the rudder blade must be made deeper or moved farther forward on the boat. In short, there are many good locations for the rudder, and they all work well if they are incorporated in a careful design.

7. *How can I remove the scratches and gouges in the gel coat on the topsides of my boat?*

Answer: If the gouges are deep enough to penetrate the gel coat, they should be cleaned and dried and then filled with epoxy putty. A smooth finish can then be obtained with wet and dry sandpaper followed by automobile rubbing compound. Minor scratches can be rubbed out with just the rubbing compound. Finally, three coats of paste wax should be applied to preserve the finish. In fact, the hull should be waxed every three months in order to maintain a high gloss and to prevent the ultraviolet rays in the sunlight from deteriorating the gel coat. If the topsides have numerous gouges and if the surface is chalky and deteriorated, it will have to be sanded and painted with a polyurethane or epoxy coating. Painting may also be desirable if the topsides have undergone a large repair that does not match the existing surface.

8. *How can I add to the depth of the keel on my powerboat?*

Answer: Very often a production powerboat has a shallow keel or no keel on the bottom, and the lowest appendage on the boat is the propeller. This design always results in damage to the propeller when the boat goes aground, and anyone who does any cruising at all will go aground now and then. A deep keel is a very worthwhile and necessary part of the design on any boat, not only to protect the propellers but also to help the boat steer a straighter course in a heavy seaway. Steering ability is especially important if you are to get effective use of an autopilot. The only boats that do not need keels are the generally smaller ones intended for racing or water skiing.

A keel can be added to a wood boat by bolting additional planks to the existing keel structure, and a keel can be added to a metal boat by welding. Here, we will discuss installing a keel on a fiberglass hull. It is not easy to laminate glass on vertical or overhead surfaces, but this is essentially what has to be done to attach a new keel to the glass hull. The glass material must be formed over a wood core into a U shape with flanges extending outboard for ten inches at the top. It is best to begin by cutting a plywood core, either three-quarters inch or one inch in thickness, and bonding it to the hull at centerline with epoxy glue. Then cover the plywood core with glass to a thickness of one inch at the bottom to one-half inch at the top flanges. The hull surface must be sanded rough before laminating to insure a good bond, and the half-inch-thick flanges on both sides are sanded so that they blend smoothly into the existing hull surface. It is good design to have a smooth curve at the intersection of the keel and the hull, using a glass putty filler or wood to form this radius of at least two inches.

9. *What is the best shape for a powerboat hull, and should it be flat or 'V' shaped in section?*

Answer: In order to define the optimum hull shape, we must first determine the speed at which the boat will be operating, and whether it will be in calm or rough water. Basically, a narrow beamed boat will have less resistance than a wider hull, and all hulls should have a very sharp 'V' in forwardmost five feet of the underbody (a narrow, fine entry). A round bilged boat with only a small amount of 'V' (deadrise) at the stern is normally best for slow speeds, and a larger amount of deadrise (about twelve degrees) works well with a chine hull ('V' bottom) at higher speeds. The 'V' bottom hulls normally have the aft one-third of the hull below the waterline of a constant shape so that the waterflow is not twisted and exits cleanly from the transom. These high speed hulls also have a chine line in profile (the intersection line of the bottom and the hull sides) that slopes upward from the transom, rather than being parallel to the waterline as designed into a medium speed hull.

These guidelines are only approximate as there are many exceptions. For example, a fishing boat or tugboat may have a very wide beam for purposes of increasing stability, and they have a deep draft and a sharp 'V' forward changing to almost a flat bottom at the transom. Also, a small fast boat operating in calm water, such as a racing or water skiing hull, may have a wide beam and an essentially flat bottom in order to create a minimum wake. If you are considering the purchase of a boat for use in specific waters, take a look at the other boats being used successfully in that area, rent one for a day, and then obtain the same shape of hull if it lives up to your expectations. Of course, the maintenance of a boat will greatly affect the reliability of performance. Be sure the bottom is free of barnacles and other marine growth, keep the engine maintenance record up-to-date, and don't operate the engine at full throttle for more than a few minutes at a time.

There is a third hull shape used in custom fabricated monohulls that also produces good performance and is primarily used to reduce costs in plywood and metal boat construction. It is called the multi-chine hull with two, three or four curved, longitudinal intersection lines along the hull surface that run continuously in a fair line from stem to stern. Either powerboat or sailboat hull shapes may be successfully produced by this method, normally for a custom hull. The technique can easily be applied to the construction of a mold for fabricating fiberglass hulls.

10. *How can I increase my fuel and water tank capacity for long cruises?*

Answer: To increase water tank capacity, you can buy one of the many brands of water makers that use the heat of the engine cooling water to distill fresh water from seawater. Or you could also consider catching rainwater. On a sailboat, an awning can be rigged to funnel rainwater into the boat's tanks, but on a powerboat it is normal to fix a permanent drain line in the lowest corner of the cabin roof. Actually, a tank fill line with a watertight cap is mounted in the roof and the cap is merely left open when the rain begins. You will have to install a solid rail around the edges of the roof to make sure all the rain drains into the fill pipe. You should also put a threaded cap in a scupper hole in the rail to drain the water to the deck when you don't need it in the tanks.

It is sometimes difficult to install extra fuel tanks in the available space under berths or in the engineroom, and flexible rubber tanks may be the solution. It is always best to locate the tanks toward the middle of the boat so there will not be any change of trim as the full tanks become empty. When the contents of a tank must be transferred into an empty existing tank, they should be pumped rather than fed by a gravity drain line from one to another. All fittings on any fuel tank must be located on the *top* of the tank to avoid the danger of a fitting leaking fuel into the bilges. It is very dangerous to carry fuel in tanks located on deck unless they are secured in permanent mountings that are bolted through the deck. Wire and rope lashings have a habit of wearing through with the motion of the boat in a seaway. Also, the center of gravity of the boat is raised with the high weights of the deck load. If tanks are carried on deck, the transfer of fuel to the permanent tanks should be done only in calm weather.

11. *Can I add a fishing cockpit to my powerboat by lengthening the boat aft of the transom?*

Answer: Fishing cockpits have been added successfully to many boats of all materials, but great care must be taken by the boat builder to insure that the existing lines of the boat—the hull shape—are extended fairly and smoothly. It is normally impractical to lengthen the boat by more than ten feet, as the beam at the new transom becomes too narrow and steering difficulties will develop. If the rudders are left in the original position, the steering sensitivity will be somewhat reduced, as the centroid of the waterline plane about which the boat turns has been moved aft, and the distance between this centroid and the rudders is reduced. Whether the rudders have to be relocated is a matter of preference and the characteristics of the individual hull.

The builder should clamp long battens to the hull over a distance of at least twelve feet, extending them aft the desired length of the addition. From these battens, temporary station frames can be made to establish permanent framing and final fairing. A cockpit addition cannot merely be bolted to the existing transom, and new longitudinal stringers will have to be secured the full length of the new cockpit, extending forward alongside the original stringers for at least ten feet. Exhaust ports in the transom will, of course, have to be extended aft to the new transom along with other auxiliary exhausts, vents, and the stern light.

12. *What type of antifouling paint should I use?*

Answer: Most major manufacturers have formulated coatings for all materials, and it is vital to choose a paint for your hull type, whether it be fiberglass, or steel, or aluminum. Be sure to keep in mind that any paints containing copper or mercury compounds must not be used with steel or aluminum hulls.

Whatever type or brand of paint you select, you must start with a clean, dry surface and apply a primer coat. Use a primer that is made specifically for the paint selected, and by the same manufacturer. Follow the instructions exactly as printed on the can, and make sure all the old paint and primer are removed unless you are positive that the previous coat is identical to the one you are about to apply.

When a fiberglass hull is new and has not previously been painted, it will have to be sanded with a medium-grit paper prior to application of the primer. This sanding removes the wax or parting agent that was used in the molding process, and if it is not removed, it will prevent adhesion of the primer.

13. *How can I tell if my boat is really seaworthy and capable of use in the ocean?*

Answer: The word *seaworthy* is a general term that is often used to describe boats in advertising brochures, but it must be defined in terms of wind strength and wave height in order to be significant. One could say that a boat is seaworthy if it does not take on water after being subjected to continuous pounding into heavy seas, although unusual wind strengths and wave heights will damage most ships no matter how many oceans they have previously crossed. After every hurricane, typhoon, or whole gale boats and ships are reported damaged or lost. Does this mean that they were not seaworthy? Or were the losses just unavoidable accidents?

Throughout this book we have emphasized thickness of laminate, stiffeners to prevent flexing, and the tightness of the deck-to-hull joint. If the boat is satisfactory in terms of these three details, the hull is well on the way to being a quality product. Of course, the rigging and hardware have to be properly installed, and the watertightness of the portlights, companionway closures, and hatches is extremely important. Everything about the boat must be designed and installed to resist the effects of fatigue or the repeated application of high loads, such as pounding into a seaway.

If a boat is used primarily on protected waters, such as rivers and small lakes, and is not used in bad weather, it will probably have a very long lifetime without serious structural problems. However, if a powerboat is run at high speeds into five-foot waves over a long period of time, one might expect the forward areas of the hull to be repeatedly stressed to the point of failure, but these same areas may not be overstressed if the boat is operated only at medium speeds. It is easy to see, therefore, that the longevity of any hull is greatly determined not only by quality construction but also by temperate operation. This same point applies to sailboats, and one sign of an experienced sailor is knowing when to carry smaller sails, whether racing or cruising.

14. *What type of boat should I buy to live aboard and possibly cruise around the world?*

Answer: So much personal preference is involved in the selection of a boat that this is a very difficult question. If you want to live aboard a boat at a marina and possibly cruise the inland rivers, you can choose from a wide selection of boats. The production power-boats manufactured in the United States offer good accommodations for the purpose, and in 1977 such a boat cruised successfully to Europe with an economical single diesel engine. The crew did carry extra fuel in inflatable tanks, and they chose the milder summertime weather. Boat length is largely a matter of individual budget, but thirty feet should be considered minimum for comfortable living aboard. Before selecting a boat, visit others who have had experience in living afloat, keeping in mind that storage space is limited and that your wardrobe and the quantities of your other personal possessions will have to be reduced in size.

When considering extensive cruising, and possibly a trip around the world, most people will consider only a motorsailer or sailboat both for the pleasure of sailing and for independence from fuel supplies. The fuel capacity is of course limited, and the engine becomes a secondary, emergency means of propulsion. Once again, the size boat selected is a matter of individual preference, but it should be realized that sailing is more comfortable in a longer boat whose displacement is kept fairly light by keeping the interior accommodation to a minimum. On the other hand, I have just talked with a couple who recently sailed around the world for four years in their thirty-three-foot fiberglass sloop without any adverse incidents. They said that they had relatively few problems with repairs, dockage, and bureaucratic paperwork because they were small, and they certainly made many friends. It is noteworthy that the boat was ten years old when they acquired it, but they made sure the hull, deck, and rigging were sound before they started on the extended trip.

It is always wise to take a new boat on a few short trips in rough weather in order to gain confidence in the integrity of the hull and rigging. It is most important to have the sails and winches arranged so that the boat is easily handled by two people, and it is always prudent to carry smaller sails when ocean cruising. Personal preference determines whether the sailboat will be a keel or centerboard model, as both types have successfully made long cruises. If you plan to cruise inland waterways, bays, and rivers, a shallow-draft centerboard boat may be a necessity.

Not only is it important to test the boat that you plan to cruise in thoroughly, but you should carry as much emergency equipment and as many spare parts as you have space for. Certainly a dinghy or inflatable boat with adequate survival provisions and water is mandatory. Repair materials for the hull, pumps, masts, and rigging are necessary, especially if they are not available in every port. It is wise to select a boat whose engine and other installed systems are sold internationally so that repair service can be found without much difficulty.

15. *Can I reduce the initial cost of a boat by buying a bare hull and deck and fitting out the interior myself?*

Answer: Yes, but only if you are very experienced both in handling boats and in working with tools. And most important, you must have a great deal of free time in which to work. What you will be saving in dollars is the cost of labor to complete the boat, and the more you do yourself, the more you will save. On the other hand, materials will probably cost you more than they would cost a builder, because you are unlikely to be able to obtain the maximum discounts that the manufacturer enjoys. And when you figure expenses, you should not forget to include the rent of the building space and the purchase of necessary tools. Most people who build their own boats take great pride in their workmanship and in the accomplishment of completing a satisfactory project. These are the motivating factors that insure a job well done, and anyone who undertakes boat building must have such motivation.

If you purchase a bare hull, the molder should install some bracing across the beam to make sure that the very flexible fiberglass hull does not bend out of shape, and this bracing must be retained until the bulkheads are secured in place. The symmetry of the sheer can be checked by fixing a string on centerline and measuring out to both sheers at the same longitudinal position.

Keep in mind the importance of wood joinerwork in contributing to the stiffness of the hull when it is securely glassed in place on both sides. As the bulkheads are installed, the necessary longitudinal stiffeners are glassed in place to further insure that a fair hull shape will be retained.

Many new boat builders find that it is much easier to build the deck if the top edges of the bulkheads are shaped to the curvature of the deck. Longitudinal beams are then set into notches in each bulkhead the full length of the boat, ensuring a fair and smooth curvature for the whole length of the deck. When building a deck, it is important first to establish the height of the deck (or trunk cabin) at the centerline of the boat. This longitudinal line of the deck at centerline can be convex, concave, or straight, but it must be smooth and continuous. Its height is determined by the headroom required above the cabin flooring.

When the bare hull is completed, it is easy to determine what you want in the interior accommodations, but clearances must be allowed for installation of the engine, tanks, plumbing, and wiring. The joinerwork can be best visualized by cutting cardboard boxes to the dimensions of the counters, berths, galley, head, and lockers and then taping them to the hull and bulkheads temporarily. You can then walk around this simulated interior to see whether everything is in the correct location before actually cutting the plywood for the permanent installation. When you are finished, it is a good idea to hire a surveyor to check every phase of construction, not only because you may have missed something, but to ascertain the integrity for your insurance company.

16. *How much weight can I carry in my boat?*

Answer: When you add weight to your boat, whether it is in the form of people, diving air tanks, or fishing gear, you normally add it in a high location that raises the center of gravity of the boat and results in a less stable hull. For this reason you must be careful about adding excessive weight, especially when it is above deck and subject to rolling to the lee side. Rough weather may produce waves that heel the boat excessively and accentuate the danger of overloading, and it is a good idea to stay in protected waters under such conditions.

A boat carrying full fuel and water, a crew of two, and reasonable equipment and stores should float at about its normal waterline. If you load the boat with extra people or equipment, be sure the weight doesn't make the boat ride more than two inches lower. To give an indication of the loads involved, a normal twenty-six-foot boat would require about 1,200 pounds (about eight people) to make it sit two inches lower in the water; a thirty-foot hull would require about 1,800 pounds; and a thirty-six-foot hull would require about 2,500 pounds. In addition to the two-inch immersion recommendation, however, it is important not to reduce the freeboard by more than one-half. For example, a powerboat may have a low cockpit with scuppers only a few inches above the waterline, and this distance from scuppers to waterline should not be reduced significantly or wave action may flood the cockpit and the bilges if the cockpit is not completely watertight.

17. *How can I estimate speed?*

Answer: Estimating the speed of a boat is a rather difficult task, as so many variables are involved. For example, the engine may not be perfectly tuned; the bottom and propeller may have a few barnacles; the boat may have a full-length keel or just a small skeg; or the through-hull fittings and other hull attachments may not be faired smoothly into the hull surface.

Actually, the only accurate method of determining boat speed is to average two or three runs over a measured mile, realizing that this gives the speed of the boat only at that time under those conditions. Figure 8 has been prepared from actual boat tests and theoretical calculations and from boat tests conducted by *Boating* magazine (Ziff-Davis Publishing Company, One Park Avenue, New York, N. Y. 10016). This table should prove sufficiently accurate for estimating speeds prior to actual trial runs of normally loaded, production powerboats.

A sailboat or a displacement speed powerboat has a hull shape and installed engine horsepower particularly suited to slower speeds; it will not approach semiplaning or planing speeds. When any boat is moving slowly, it develops a bow wave and a stern wave that become larger as the boat speed increases. The boat then travels in the trough between these two waves, just as if it were in a natural ocean wave with the crests at the bow and stern. Since the boat does not have sufficient power to climb over its bow wave, its speed is limited by the speed of the wave that the hull displaces. It has been observed that this limiting, or displacement, speed (measured in knots) is 1.34 multiplied by the square root of the waterline length of the hull. This calculation applies for all sailboats. Boat designers have more complicated methods of estimating the resistance characteristics of new hulls and calculating the maximum speeds, but the use of Figure 8 will give very similar results.

18. *What type of bilge pump should I install in my boat?*

Answer: Every boat should have at least one manual pump of at least ten gallons per minute capacity. It can be permanently mounted

FIGURE 8
Approximate Speeds of Powerboats in Miles Per Hour

Total Brake Horsepower (rows) × Boat Weight in Pounds (columns)

Total Brake Horsepower	4,000	5,000	6,000	7,000	8,000	9,000	10,000	11,000	12,000	13,000	14,000	15,000	16,000	17,000	18,000	19,000	20,000	21,000
700				45	43.5	41.8	40.4	39.2	37.8	36.4	35	34	33.1	32.3	31.5	30.7	29.8	29
600			45	43	41.4	39.8	38.2	36.6	35	34	33	32.2	31.5	30.7	30	29.2	28.5	27.8
550			44	42	40.1	38.4	36.8	35	33.9	33	32.1	31.3	30.5	29.7	28.9	28.1	27.3	26.5
500		45	43	41	39	37	35	33.4	32.2	31.1	30.4	29.6	28.8	28	27.2	26.4	25.6	24.8
450	45	43.5	41	39	37	35	33	32	31	30	29	28.1	27.2	26.4	25.6	24.8	24	23.4
400	43.4	42	39	37	35	33	31	30	29	28.3	27.5	26.7	25.9	25.1	24.3	23.5	23	22.2
350	42	40.2	37	35	33	31	29	28	27	26.1	25.3	24.5	23.7	22.7	22	21.2	20.5	19.8
300	42	38	35	33	30	28	27	26	25	23.7	23.3	23	22	21	20	19	18	17
250	38	35	33	31	29	27	25	24	22.2	21.1	20.4	19.7	19	18.3	17.6	17	16.3	15.7
200	35	31	28	26	25	24	23	21.5	20	18.5	17	16.5	16	15.5	15	14.8	14.6	14.4
150	30	27	24	22.7	21.5	20.2	19	18	17.5	16	15	14.7	14.4	14.1	13.8	13.6	13.4	13.2
100	25	23	20	17	16	15	14.8	14.5	14.2	14	13.7	13.5	13.2	13	12.7	12.5	12.3	12

Boat Weight in Pounds

with an overboard discharge, or it can be portable but with a long discharge hose that will reach the cockpit scuppers or over the sheer rail. In a sailboat, it is especially important to have the pump discharge located high enough so that it will not be under water when the boat is at an angle of heel. It is normally most convenient to have the through-hull fitting for the pump discharge in the transom on centerline, but in many sailboats the pump and the cockpit drain line are connected, as they both serve the same purpose and one hull opening is eliminated.

Most owners like the convenience of electric bilge pumps, as they can be used with an automatic float switch to clear the bilges when the boat is unattended. However, the switch should also be wired to a warning light or buzzer to indicate when the pump is operating. If an unusually large amount of water is on board, this warning will show that the pump is running continuously and that the boat requires attention before the batteries are fully discharged. Many electric pumps are of small capacity and are really only suited for water pressure systems, so it is a good idea to check your pump to make sure it has a capacity of at least ten gallons per minute.

In well-designed boats, all portions of the bilge drain to one low point, or to a bilge sump tank, but if the sump area is subdivided by watertight bulkheads, there will have to be a bilge pump in each watertight section of the hull. In an emergency, you can remove the engine cooling water intake hose from its through-hull fitting and insert it into the bilgewater. Close the intake valve first, of course. Then run the engine and let it pump the bilgewater through the cooling system and overboard. If you really have a large amount of water in the boat, it is sometimes best simply to use a bucket and empty the water into the cockpit. Many sailors have reported that this is the most efficient way to empty the bilges!

19. *How can I repair bulkheads that are loose at the hull?*

Answer: The plywood bulkheads are usually attached to the hull with a fiberglass overlay of mat and woven roving. If the two surfaces are not clean, or if the glass hull has not been sanded thoroughly,

106

this secondary bond of the plywood to the hull may be poor and will be subject to delamination as the hull is twisted and pounded by wave action. If this has happened, the old glass can be removed with a thin chisel intended for steel, followed by sanding of both the wood and the hull on both sides of the bulkhead. The bulkhead is then reattached by alternating two layers each of mat and woven roving on both sides to a minimum width of six inches on each surface. Make sure that the top edge is secured to the underside of the deck and the cabin top in a similar manner. It is very important that the bottom edge of the bulkhead be made watertight with resin and glass to prevent bilgewater from being soaked into the edge grain of the plywood. If the counters, cabinetry, and other joinerwork have come loose from the bulkhead, the two can be refastened with epoxy glue on the edges and glass overlay underneath where it will not show. One or two bulkheads may loosen because of careless installation, as described above, or all the bulkheads may eventually loosen, which is a sign of insufficient framing between the bulkheads. If the latter is the case, the hull needs more longitudinal frames spaced about twenty inches apart and with a depth of two inches.

20. *My sailboat mast is stepped on deck. When the boat is under sail, I can't open the door to the head. What can be done?*

Answer: This situation, common on sailboats, results when the bulkhead and mast support have not been fastened tightly to the underside of the deck. The mast load pushes the cornerpost and door framing out of alignment, causing the door to bind in the frame. The load of the mast is intended to be taken by the heavy cornerpost, but this can occur only if the post is tightly secured to the underside of the deck at the top and to the inside of the hull at the bottom. Usually, this problem occurs on boats with a one-piece molded glass headliner that completely covers the underside of the deck (or cabin top) and prevents access for securing the deck and the top of the bulkhead. It doesn't do much good to bond the headliner and bulkhead together as you can't be sure that the headliner is secured to the deck! This problem does not occur when the mast is stepped on the keel.

107

If the boat has no headliner, you can glass the top of the bulkhead and cornerpost to the underside of the deck without difficulty, after sanding both surfaces. Bond the components on both sides by alternating three layers of mat and three of woven roving, finishing with an additional layer of mat in order to present a smooth appearance. After this installation, you can match the existing finish of the overhead in color and materials.

If the boat has a headliner, scribe the line of the bulkhead top on the headliner and cut away the headliner, forming a slot slightly wider than the bulkhead thickness. This is a tedious job and can probably best be accomplished by drilling a series of holes in the headliner, being careful not to drill into the deck laminate. After this slot has been cut, bond the deck, the headliner, and the top of the bulkhead together with a wide, thick application of polyester putty. The seam can be hidden with a quarter-round wood molding fastened with epoxy glue.

The deck (or cabin top) should also be checked to see that the laminate is solid and that a core material was not used mistakenly in the area of the mast step. Before the top of the supporting bulkhead is secured, drill some small holes about one-quarter inch deep from the top of the deck and look for a core material. Solid wood or plywood is acceptable in this area, but balsa wood and foam do not have the compressive strength to be located under a mast step. If you find a core, the bottom plate on the mast step should be through-bolted to another plate located under the deck and on top of the bulkhead and cornerpost. Between these plates and around each bolt there should be short lengths of aluminum pipe the same length as the deck thickness. These pipe bushings will take most of the mast load and transfer it to the supporting post and structure underneath.

If you find a solid laminate under the mast step, check it for delamination by pushing up on the bottom side of the deck with a small jack and checking to see that the top of the deck starts to flex at the same time as the bottom laminate. If not, there apparently has been some delamination, which can be repaired by injecting epoxy glue through the small holes drilled into the top of the deck.

21. *Where should the straps be placed on the hull for hauling out with a traveling hoist?*

Answer: Most powerboats and sailboats are ruggedly constructed along the centerline so that hauling out presents no structural problem. This lifting, however, stresses the hull laminate more than almost anything else that happens to the boat. Of course, the two straps should be located an equal distance forward and aft of the center of gravity of the hull, and in an area where the strap is not on the rudder, propeller, shaft, or strut. It is convenient to have a scale drawing showing the underwater shape of the hull (docking plan) or to have some marking on the rub rail to show where the straps must be located.

In the early days of fiberglass boats, narrow keel sections with too thin a laminate failed on both powerboats and sailboats when they were hauled out. But the manufacturers soon learned that any hollow, unstiffened keel section must have extra layers of laminate. This problem was particularly prevalent in the after areas of sailboat keels, aft of the ballast, where there was a narrow section either hollow or filled with foam. These are difficult areas to inspect, and about all the surveyor can do is scrape away the paint in a few spots on the outside of the bottom of the keel to see if the laminate has previously been crushed during haul-out.

22. *How can I add a rub rail to my boat?*

Answer: A rub rail certainly is a convenience on any boat, as a concrete or creosoted wood piling can really make a mess of a glass hull. The rub rail should be wide enough to protect the hull where its beam is widest and its bottom edge should taper upward and outboard so that it will not become lodged on top of a low piling.

A sheer fender, or rub rail, can be made of wood, pipe, extruded aluminum, extruded rubber, or even old fire hose. All of these are acceptable for the job, and the material is a matter of personal preference. Whatever is installed, however, it will have to be bolted through the fiberglass hull. This is sometimes a tedious job if the interior of the hull at the sheer is covered with a hull liner. Depending on the installation, it may be better to bolt right through this liner rather than remove it. In any case, large washers must be used under the nuts, and the hole through the hull must be filled with bedding compound as the bolt is inserted.

If you find that the hull laminate thickness at the bolt holes is less than one-quarter inch, more laminate should be added in the sheer area to at least that thickness. This extra overlay should bond to both the deck and the hull, as both are structural laminates that serve to distribute the load when the rub rail is hit against a dock piling.

23. *How can I stop water leaks from the deck-to-hull joint?*

Answer: Try to isolate the location of these leaks by inspecting the interior all along the joint area. Streaks of dirty water or rust will usually reveal where the water has penetrated, although the exterior point of water entry may be some distance from these spots. For this reason, it is always best to remove the fastenings, rails, and exterior hardware for a distance of three feet on either side of the water entry. The seam where the deck meets the hull may be covered by a rub rail on the side of the hull or by a toerail on deck, and the head of the bolt may be difficult to reach, thus making it easier to remove the nut from the inside and lift the rail away from the hull to provide access to the edges of the deck and hull for caulking. If the edges of the laminate are found to be flexible and without resin, the glass should be dried thoroughly and saturated with epoxy glue. This prevents water from seeping into the glass laminate.

Before replacing the rub rail, use a good marine bedding compound between the rail and the glass, between the two glass laminates, and in every bolt hole. Then, when the bolts are tightened, the compound should squeeze from every hole and block any water entry. The threads on each bolt should be staked to prevent loosening. Complete the job by applying two layers of mat and woven roving to the inside of the joint area. Probably the most difficult part of this procedure is getting access to the inside of the hull at the sheer, as there may be a solid glass hull liner and headliner in the way. If this is the situation, the liner must be cut away with a sabre saw and later replaced with a teak strip to cover the sawed seam.

24. *How can I stop the portlights from leaking?*

Answer: Some years ago, the boating industry was plagued with a few manufacturers who were installing portlights with no fastenings and just a little polyester resin. Some were also installing their cleats and lifeline stanchion bases with one bolt and three screws. All of these installations will eventually leak as the boat twists in a seaway and the laminate flexes around the hardware. There is only one way to install hardware correctly, and that is with bolts, nuts, large washers, and plenty of bedding compound. Keep in mind that if the laminate has a balsa wood or foamed plastic core, you will not be able to tighten the bolts completely unless there is a pipe sleeve around each bolt to prevent the core from being crushed. Of course, you must put a large backing plate under the cleat or any deck fitting, and use large washers with the bolts.

In order to improve the appearance of the inside of the portlight, a trim ring is used instead of washers, and acorn nuts are used to hide the ends of the bolts. A few boats have nonopening portlights without a metal frame. Instead, the safety glass is held onto the cabin side with a rubber extrusion. The rubber usually deteriorates over the years, resulting in leaking windows, and replacement parts for these boats have not been available. One solution to this problem is bolting a quarter-inch-thick piece of plastic over the window opening, using plenty of bedding compound, to make a permanent installation.

25. *How can I add another lower shroud to my sailboat?*

Answer: Many production sailboats under thirty-five feet in length have only one lower shroud installed on each side of the boat to reduce costs. This rig may be perfectly adequate from the standpoint of strength required to support the mast, but one shroud does not provide sufficient fore-and-aft bracing for the center of the mast.

Two lower shrouds on each side of the boat is always the preferred installation. When adding a shroud, it is probably best to duplicate the materials and the type of installation already on the boat. Locate each new shroud chainplate about eighteen inches forward or eighteen inches aft of the upper shroud (depending on which shroud needs to be added). This dimension is not critical, but never put a lower shroud less than twelve inches from the upper shroud.

It is probably easiest to put a new shroud chainplate on the outside of the hull. Increase the laminate thickness in the area, and through-bolt the chainplate, using a large backing plate on the inside. The extra glass material should be about eighteen by thirty inches and consist of three layers of mat alternating with three layers of woven roving. The backing plate, which can be aluminum, should be 50 percent wider than the stainless steel chainplate. The thickness of each plate should be the same as the diameter of the wire rope shroud.

If you don't particularly care to have the chainplates show on the outside of the hull, they can go through the deck and be bolted to an existing partial bulkhead or to a glass-over-plywood knee that is heavily overlaid to the hull and the underside of the deck.

Finally, the shroud chainplate may be bolted through the deck only, but this installation is not recommended for boats over thirty feet in length, and even in smaller boats the deck-to-hull connection must be heavily reinforced in order to distribute the load adequately to the hull. The use of padeyes or stainless steel U-bolts as chainplates, bolted through the deck, is recommended only when the supporting structure under the deck has been calculated by an experienced designer. (See Chapter 4 for further structural recommendations.)

26. *Can I install inboard scuppers so that the topsides will not become streaked with dirty water?*

Answer: Many production boats have drain holes through the toerail so that rainwater will run off the deck, but this does cause the topsides to become dirty. In order to circumvent this problem, you can install 1½-inch-diameter scuppers just inboard of the sheer with a drain hose and four stainless steel hose clamps leading to a "T" connection in another, already installed, drain hose. A sink drain or cockpit scupper hose would be very convenient for this purpose, if it has a properly installed seacock and through-hull fitting.

Some quality boats have another type of deck scupper that is integral with the hull—the inside of the hull forms one side of a water duct from the deck down to about one foot above the waterline. This duct is formed by laminating glass in a tubular shape from the underside of the deck scupper, down the side of the hull, to a hole through the hull. Since this method relies on the secondary bonding of the glass to the hull, it is best done by a manufacturer when building the boat rather than at some later date. Great care must be taken in making this tube, as the hull must be sanded clean and epoxy resin used in the lamination to insure a watertight connection.

The location of the scuppers on deck, and the total number, depend largely on the slope of the surface. Most boats have at least three drains on each side, one at the lowest point, and one about six feet both forward and aft of the first drain. The low point will change with different conditions of loading, especially water and fuel, and it is well to have two extra scuppers rather than one too few. A sailboat will normally trim down by the bow as it heels, as the forward sections of the hull are much finer than the afterbody. For this reason, an extra scupper should be located about amidships. Also, it is best to have two scuppers located forward in the cockpit footwell, but the offshore sailor will want two scuppers at the aft end in addition. On the same subject, it is good practice to look for cockpit seat drains along the outboard edges. Nothing is more uncomfortable than to sit in water collecting in the corner of a lee seat.

27. *How can I reinforce a springy deck?*

Answer: Let's assume that the too-flexible deck is forward, over the V-berths, and that the distance between bulkheads is about seventy-five inches. Also, we are presuming that the deck was made only slightly below the required thickness rather than exceedingly thin. A normal deck may have a laminate of a three-quarter-inch balsa wood core with fiberglass faces three-sixteenths of an inch thick on both sides. A substantially thinner deck may require additional laminate plus deck beams. The thickness can be checked at one of the hardware fastening holes. We are assuming that the addition of a post, located between bulkheads, would interfere with the accommodations, and that deck beams are required in order to stiffen the deck.

Any headliner will have to be removed, but it will be replaced later by fastening it to the new deck beams. The core, or form, for the new beams can be cut from half-inch plywood. The upper edge must be curved to the deck, and the lower edge should be cut to a depth of two inches on centerline and eight inches at each sheer. After this core is glued to the underside of the deck with epoxy glue, it is covered with three layers of mat, alternating with three layers of woven roving on both sides, and overlapping the deck about four inches. In this example, there would be two beams spaced about twenty-five inches apart.

If you cannot tolerate the loss of two inches of headroom at centerline, you could locate the beams longitudinally, spaced twenty-four inches apart, with each end set into notches in the bulkheads. The plywood core can be one and one-half inches deep and covered with the same laminate.

28. *I can see light through the glass hull. Is this normal?*

Answer: Fiberglass laminate is translucent, and strong light will be visible from the inside of the hull in most boats. The color gel coat on the outside and the painted interior will block out the light to some extent, depending on the paint thickness, but it is perfectly normal for the hull to transmit light. The resin, which comprises about 70 percent of the laminate, is the translucent component. Most manufacturers try to cover the hull interior for this reason, just for cosmetic purposes, but the light transmission has nothing to do with the structural integrity of the boat.

The surveyor should take advantage of this property of the laminate in order to inspect the hull more thoroughly for inherent defects wherever the inside of the hull is uncovered. The translucency is also used to good advantage in fiberglass tanks; a vertical strip is left unpainted on the side of the tank so that one can see the level of the liquid inside.

29. *Should I get a boat with a smaller cockpit for ocean sailing?*

Answer: If you are making long ocean passages, there is always a possibility that large waves may break at the crests and water will be thrown on deck and into the cockpit. We are concerned with the problems of preventing water from entering the interior of the boat and removing any water from the cockpit footwell as quickly as possible. Of course, the hatches and portlights should be watertight, but special attention should be given to the cockpit seat lockers, which can be continuously soaked by waves and spray. Not only should the lockers have gaskets and tight-fitting latches, but all three edges should have drain grooves so that the water is directed toward the scuppers in the footwell. It is best to have four footwell scuppers, one and one-half inches in diameter, led to the seacocks so that they will drain when the boat is at an extreme angle of heel.

For long ocean passages, it is well to keep the portlights securely fastened at all times and to keep all hatches except the main companionway opening closed. This latter hatch should be protected by a canvas dodger to ward off freak waves and to provide some spray shield for the helmsman. Any opening under the companionway hatch should not extend below deck level, which is normally about eighteen inches above the cockpit footwell. When in port and on protected waters, it is nice to have a large, comfortable cockpit, but in heavy weather, it is well to keep this large space from filling with water. Both these requirements can be fulfilled by temporarily lashing blocks of foamed plastic in the cockpit so that its volume will be reduced for ocean cruising. Other materials could be used for lightweight, high-volume flotation, but foam seems the most inexpensive solution. In some cases, a canvas can be lashed across the cockpit coamings to deflect the water overboard rather than into the footwell and scuppers.

30. *How can I determine the value of my boat?*

Answer: The price of any boat depends on many constantly changing variables. Unless a person is directly involved with boat brokerage, he will have difficulty determining the price level at any particular time. You could scan magazines and newspaper advertisements and check with boat brokers, but you still may not find the true selling price of your boat, as the advertised, or asking, price may be grossly inflated in an attempt to get the highest price for the seller.

I have found the most reliable source of boat prices to be boat directories, such as the one published by BUC International Corporation, 1881 Northeast 26th Street, Fort Lauderdale, Florida 33305. They employ statistical analysis of boats that have actually been sold throughout the United States and have listings for each boat, both new and used, from every manufacturer.

From 1972 to 1979 there was a decided disparity of economic conditions in different parts of this country, and market prices were subject to varying pressures. The result has been a confusing pricing structure in all areas of merchandising, especially recreational boating. The costs of raw materials such as petroleum-derived polyester resins have been consistently rising, but in some areas high unemployment has resulted in lower retail sales and price levels. All these factors are taken into consideration by BUC International Corporation and presented in a price correction table called an area scale that is applied to the listed price range for each boat in their directory.

It is no longer valid to use an annual percentage depreciation to arrive at the value of a used boat. In fact, in the five years prior to 1978, most boats did not show any depreciation of value! Of course, much of this stability of price can be attributed to inflation. Also, much of the expense of owning a boat, and much of the resultant value, depend on maintenance, which is not taken into account in any depreciation schedule. For this reason alone, it is worthwhile to have the boat checked by a competent surveyor, who can ascertain the condition of the hull and equipment. The impartial survey report can be a valuable selling instrument for either buyer or seller, but one should look to the broker for price comparisons with similar boats having similar installed equipment, as the surveyor is not normally familiar with the prices of all the boats that have been sold in his locality.

Some magazines and some boat sales people have attempted to compare boats by figuring their cost per pound of total weight. This may be an interesting comparison for new boats in one particular model year, but as a rule of thumb it is not valid from one year to another, and the dollar value per pound must be constantly changed. This pricing method is definitely not reasonable for used boats, because equipment of various weights is added over the life of the boat. Additions may be very light in weight but expensive—electronics and life rafts are good examples. The statistical price study is certainly the preferred technique of determining boat values.

31. *Exactly what is the surveyor looking for?*

Answer: When the surveyor is on his hands and knees with his nose close to a piece of deck hardware, many owners wonder just what is he inspecting so closely. In fact, I have had an owner selling his boat ask sarcastically, "You don't have to look for lint, do you?" As mentioned previously, the surveyor must look very closely at every square inch of the hull and deck, both inside and out to find the source of possible trouble. In the case of hardware, the bolts need be checked for tightness and the entire surface inspected for hairline cracks, twisting out of shape, and corrosion.

The surveyor might spend fifteen minutes just at the bow of the boat looking at the following items. There may be small cracks and gouges in the gel coat around the rub rail where the boat has hit a dock piling. The fastenings for the bow rail may be loose. If we are inspecting a sailboat, the headstay chainplate should be tightly bolted through the stem with a toggle installed between the chainplate and the turnbuckle. Cotter pins should be checked in the turnbuckle body and in the clevis pins. The swaged eye fitting at the end of the wire rope headstay and the entire turnbuckle should be checked for hairline cracks as well as corrosion. Often, the navigation lights are located on the bow and should be checked for operation and watertightness along with other installed hardware such as cleats, chocks and anchor windlass. It is usually difficult to determine the watertightness of the deck to hull joint from the exterior, but sometimes a loose or cracked toerail will show a surveyor where to look for water leaks on the interior. All of the above items are found on the first four feet of boat length and an equally long list can be compiled for each succeeding area of the deck and hull.

32. *What do I need to equip my boat properly?*

Answer: The volume and importance of marine accessories and equipment form an industry in itself and the owner's decisions what to purchase are just as complex. It might be logical to consider the priority of equipment by classifying it as required for safe operation, necessary for use in case of accident, or desirable but not absolutely necessary. The following list is presented only as a guide and may not be complete for all boats or cruising areas.

Equipment Required for Safe Operation

1. At least two fire extinguishers in operating condition.
2. Two horns that operate independently.
3. An approved life jacket for each person.
4. A boarding ladder that can be secured to the boat and which extends at least two feet below waterline.
5. A bell.
6. Proper ventilation for the engine compartment with outside openings that will not allow water to enter the engineroom in rough seas.
7. Proper navigation lights with spare parts.
8. If offshore, a safety harness for each person.
9. At least two bilge pumps. One should be manually operated. At least two rigid buckets.

10. All hatches and companionways should be of watertight construction.
11. Sea cocks on all through-hull fittings.
12. At least three, plastic, watertight flashlights.
13. A permanently mounted, compensated compass at the helm position plus a spare compass.
14. Lifelines, or solid rails, 24 inches high should be installed all around the boat.
15. Two anchors and secure stowage brackets.
16. A large, well stocked first aid kit, as recommended by your doctor.
17. A radar reflector with provision for mounting at the highest point of the boat.
18. Navigational charts and a method of speed indication. If a powerboat, a chart relating engine rpm with speed can be prepared by running the boat over a measured mile course.
19. A fathometer, or leadline, as desired.
20. Shut-off valves on fuel tanks and on galley stove.

Equipment Necessary in Case of Accident

1. An optional method of steering should be carried. This can include a tiller secured at the top of the rudderpost if the steering system fails and a steering oar in case the rudder itself is lost.
2. Tools and spare parts for all equipment on board.
3. Radio transmitter and receiver as determined by the area of operation, each with a separate antenna.
4. A dinghy or inflatable boat with oars and a canvas cover. Canned food and bottled water should be permanently secured to the dinghy.
5. A flare gun and ten flares.
6. An E.P.I.R.B. (emergency position indicating radio beacon) to be secured to the dinghy.
7. Underwater epoxy putty, wood plugs, plywood patches and fiberglass mat for repairing hull damage.
8. A collision mat with four lines to slide over a crack in the hull.
9. A spare propeller.
10. A horseshoe life ring with a man overboard pole and float.

Desirable Equipment

1. Electric refrigeration.
2. 110 VAC power supply generator.
3. Anchor windlass.
4. Hot water and a pressure water system.
5. Cabin heating system, and air conditioning.
6. Hand bearing compass.
7. Radar and an Omega receiver.
8. A radio direction finder.
9. Windshield wipers and washers. (Since salt spray leaves a film on the glass and will eventually scratch the windshield, a manually operated fresh water spray is desirable.)
10. If the boat does not have a permanent roof over the steering station, most people will eventually want a canvas top for protection from the hot sun or the cold winds.
11. If you have a sailboat for racing, a wind telltale at the masthead is a valuable aid and an electronic wind direction indicator helps a helmsman racing at night.

33. *What is involved in working with a yacht designer?*

Answer: The yacht designer (or naval architect, marine architect, boat designer, etc.) will design a complete custom boat or will advise the owner on small problems of repair or alteration. When consulting on a problem of propeller size, repowering, adding a bowsprit, or changing a sail plan, he will normally charge on an hourly basis. The preparation of drawings for a custom design are usually undertaken for a fixed fee.

The custom boat is desired by an owner who can't find exactly what he wants on the production boat market or who enjoys the pride of ownership of a boat designed exactly to his specifications. Since the custom hull will not be fabricated in a mold, and since the interior craftsmanship will probably be of a better quality than one sees on the showroom floor, the cost of building will probably be fifty to eighty percent more than a production model. The wide range of cost

120

is primarily affected by the materials required and the amount of hand finishing necessary on the interior joinerwork. The designer will prepare all the necessary drawings and written specifications and will assist the owner in selecting a builder if desired. Normally three preliminary drawings are submitted to various builders for quotations on construction costs and it is important to send with these drawings a list of installed equipment and type of materials to be used for the interior joinerwork. Once the construction has started, the builder and owner are usually in constant communication with the designer, but any visits by the designer to the builder's yard are not usually included in the design fee and are billed separately.

Some of the drawings that the designer provides are as follows:

Outboard profile.
Inboard profile and Arrangement Plan.
Deck Plans and Sail Plan. Interior Sections.
Drawing of the lines of the boat and table of offsets.
Calculations of curves of form and stability.
Weight calculations and power requirements.
Construction plan, profile and details.
Drawings of the engineroom arrangement and tanks.

CHAPTER 7

Repairs

One of the many advantages of fiberglass is that it can be repaired by anyone with basic hand tools. The materials can be conveniently carried on any boat, and, since glass hulls are accepted worldwide, replacement materials and assistance are available in almost every country. In fact, the ease of laminate repair is probably responsible for the widespread information that is available on repair techniques. It seems that every marine supply store, resin retailer, bookstore, and even auto supply store sells books and pamphlets on how to work with resin and woven glass materials. For this reason, we will just mention the highlights that should be common knowledge for every boat owner and surveyor.

The most common type of repair—covering and polishing fine hairline cracks in the gel coat—is really cosmetic rather than structural. It requires a great deal of patience but can be accomplished by any boat owner. These cracks result from localized stresses around hardware and normally do not represent a structural deficiency unless allowed to progress to a depth greater than the gel coat. The procedure for repair is identical to that for surface air bubbles that leave a void between the laminate and the gel coat. These bubbles are easily detected, as the gel coat collapses when touched, exposing the laminate beneath.

In both of these situations, you should grind the gel coat away to more solid material, but not so deeply as to penetrate the laminate. Next, use a polyester resin putty to completely fill the void or crack. This putty consists of resin, a filler, and chopped strands of glass, and it should be applied flush with the surrounding surface. After

123

sanding the filler smooth, apply the colored resin and wet sand it until perfectly smooth. Complete the work with rubbing compound and wax to produce a showroom finish, blending in with the surrounding area.

If there is a hole or large crack in the hull, the edges will have to be ground back to a solid laminate and tapered away from the hole for a distance of about six inches. A backing plate consisting of nothing more than waxed paper over a thin veneer taped in place outside should retain the shape of the first plies of laminate. However, with large holes, you will have to brace the backing plate with long battens bent to the fair hull shape and secured at the ends by heavy framing.

After sanding the inside of the hull clean, apply the first layer of mat laminate in the hole. Increase the area of laminate as the thickness increases. After three layers of mat have been applied, the remaining laminate can consist of alternating plies of mat and woven roving. The final thickness of the hull in the repair area should be about 50 percent greater than the original, and it never hurts to add additional framing of one-inch by three-inch stiffeners across the repair area. When this laminate has cured, the backing plate can be removed and the surface finished exactly as described for hairline cracks in the gel coat.

Many times the entire outside surface of the hull is scratched and chipped from rubbing against the dock, and complete filling, sanding, and painting is required. This is a long and tedious job that is best left to the professional yacht refinisher unless you like to spend many hours working on your boat. For extensive repairs or refinishing, it is well to obtain price quotations from several reputable boatyards, as it is very difficult to estimate fiberglass repairs accurately, and the bids may vary widely. In this regard, the surveyor will often be asked his estimate of yard repairs, and it is the wise surveyor who says he can't possibly estimate how long someone else is going to take to do the job. The reason for having a surveyor inspect the boat, of course, is to determine the condition of the hull and to list exactly what repairs must be accomplished. The surveyor is put in a difficult position if he is asked to become involved in the cost and technique of repairs.

If the hull or deck is of core construction, the repair problem becomes even more tedious and time-consuming. Most difficult is the situation in which the outside laminate is fractured but the inside laminate is untouched on a portion of the deck. In such a case, the repair is normally made from the outside of the deck, as it is very difficult to laminate on an overhead surface from the interior of the boat. Remove the core material in the area of the hole and taper the edges of the hole with a sander from the inside toward the outside to provide a surface to bond the new laminate. Lay glass mat against the intact, interior (bottom) laminate, up the edge of the core, and over the tapered portion of the outside skin. Continue this procedure until a solid laminate is installed where the old core was located. Then finish the surface in the normal manner with polyester putty and plenty of sanding. If the deck has a molded nonskid pattern, it will be almost impossible to match this texture, and the best you can do is to sand the repaired area in an acceptable shape of a rectangle or square and use a paint manufactured for nonskid decks. If the core laminate is in the hull, it is easier to make the repair from the inside, overlapping the new plies inside the inner laminate, as this surface does not have to be perfectly smooth. After building up the solid glass material inside the hole, finish the exterior surface as previously described.

As noted earlier, it is very common for a fiberglass boat to have gouges and cracks near the bottom of the keel from going aground, and like any other glass repair, these gouges must be filled to prevent water from entering the laminate. However, it is important to dry out the damaged areas thoroughly so that the resin and glass will adhere to the existing laminate. Here too, the raw, broken edges can be tapered with a sander before applying mat and woven roving over the entire area. The new laminate can be laid over the keel for a distance of twenty to thirty inches to reinforce the bottom laminate, and since this is well below the waterline, only a small amount of tapering of the plies of the laminate is necessary.

Most glass repairs will involve the above-mentioned procedures, requiring a great deal of patience but only average skills and equipment. Probably the most important point to remember is that the old laminate must be clean, dry, and free from any oil or perspiration before the repair is started.

If you operate in an area of shallow water and are frequently touching the bottom, you can prevent the bottom of the fiberglass keel from becoming gouged by adding a strip of wood. This can be accomplished by cutting a plank to the shape of the keel, about one inch thick, and applying it to the clean, sanded glass with a sealing compound that has good adhesive properties, or with epoxy glue. This sacrificial wood strip may have to be replaced frequently, but it will preserve the integrity of the glass, and keep repairs to the minimum.

Index